The Idols of Silence

Also by Anthony Slide:

BOOKS
Early American Cinema
The Griffith Actresses

PAMPHLETS
Sir Michael Balcon
Lillian Gish

The Idols of Silence

Anthony Slide

SOUTH BRUNSWICK AND NEW YORK: A. S. BARNES AND COMPANY
LONDON: THOMAS YOSELOFF LTD

© 1976 by A.S.Barnes and Co., Inc.

A.S.Barnes and Co., Inc.
Cranbury, New Jersey 08512

Thomas Yoseloff Ltd.
108 New Bond Street
London W1Y OQX, England

Library of Congress Cataloging in Publication Data

Slide, Anthony.
    The idols of silence.

    Includes bibliographies.
    1. Moving-picture actors and actresses — United
States — Biography. 2. Moving-pictures, Silent — His-
tory.
I. Title
PN1998.A2S56   791.43'028'0922   73-125
ISBN 0-498-01611-0

PRINTED IN THE UNITED STATES OF AMERICA

For Madame Olga Petrova

When old age shall this generation waste.
Thou shalt remain....
John Keats

Contents

ACKNOWLEDGMENTS 9

PART I. *The Trailblazers*

1 Mignon Anderson 15
2 Hobart Bosworth 19
3 Billie Rhodes 25
4 Kathlyn Williams 31

PART II. *The Idols of the Teens*

5 Elmer Clifton 39
6 Olga Petrova 47
7 Henry B. Walthall 56

PART III. *The Stars of the Twenties*

8 Priscilla Bonner 67
9 Bebe Daniels and Ben Lyon 75
10 Jetta Goudal 85
11 Ralph Graves 94
12 Alice Terry 99

PART IV. *The Fan Magazines: Their Stories and Their Writers*

13 The Fan Magazines 109
14 Adele Whitely Fletcher 111
15 Ruth Waterbury 115

CHECKLISTS 119

Acknowledgments

Much of the research for this volume was undertaken over a number of years with no particular plan in mind, least of all publication in a book such as this. It is, therefore, difficult to acknowledge everyone who, perhaps, should be acknowledged. The following, however, deserve special mention:

The Academy of Motion Picture Arts and Sciences (especially Alice Mitchell and Mildred Simpson)
The British Film Institute (especially Elaine Burrows and Patricia Coward)
Robert B. Cushman
Tom Fulbright
Sam Gill
Robert R. Gitt
The Library of Congress (especially David Parker, Pat Sheehan and Paul Spehr)
The Los Angeles County Museum of Natural History (John Dewar)
The Museum of Modern Art (especially Eileen Bowser and Charles Silver)
Marian Blackton Trimble
Edward Wagenknecht

I wish to thank the following stars and supporting players of this volume for their co-operation:

Mignon Anderson
Priscilla Bonner
Bebe Daniels
Adele Whitely Fletcher
Jetta Goudal
Ralph Graves
Harold Grieve
Ben Lyon
Olga Petrova
Billie Rhodes
Adela Rogers St. Johns
Alice Terry
Ruth Waterbury

The Idols of Silence

PART I.

The Trailblazers

1

Mignon Anderson

Little has been written about the studios of early companies, such as Vitagraph, Kalem, and Essanay, or their leading ladies, Florence Turner, Gene Gauntier, and Beverly Bayne. Even less mention has been made of the Thanhouser Company and its leading lady, Mignon Anderson. This is quite surprising considering that Miss Anderson was not only a charming little actress, but that she is also very much alive and well today, living in a small apartment across the way from the Burbank Studios of Warner Brothers and Columbia.

Born in Baltimore, Maryland, Miss Anderson was the daughter of actor-parents; her father was Frank Anderson, a prominent stage actor, who died in 1914. Not surprisingly, she began her career at the age of six months, when she was carried on stage by Margaret Mather. As a child actress, Mignon played with Richard Mansfield, Julia Marlowe, and Joseph Jefferson, among others. She was then packed off to schools in Brooklyn and Long Island.

After completing school, Mignon recalls, "I started posing for clothes, and I met people who were working in the picture business, who were also posing for clothes. I was invited to go to the Thanhouser Company and meet Mr. Thanhouser,

because, in those days, I was supposed to look like Mary Pickford—I really didn't. That's what the Thanhouser advertised me as, 'The Second Mary Pickford.' I started right in, and I was put under contract, and stayed with them for six years.''

The Thanhouser Company was founded in 1908 by Edwin Thanhouser, the operator of a highly successful stage company in Milwaukee. The company's studios were located, in the words of the George M. Cohan song, "only forty-five minutes from Broadway," in New Rochelle. It was to these studios that Mignon Anderson came in 1910.

Of her work at Thanhouser, Mignon Anderson remembers:

"There was just one main studio, and there were sets. There might be a set over there with a company working, and there'd be another one over here with a company working. In those days in New Rochelle, if there was a fire* in the town, and you were home, they'd ring your telephone, and you'd have to get to the studio as fast as you could. They'd take you to the fire, and they'd work a story around it.

*It is possible that Miss Anderson is recalling the disastrous fire of January 13, 1913, which destroyed the Thanhouser studios, and which was partially filmed by Thanhouser, and incorporated into one of their film releases.

Mignon Anderson (circa 1914).

Mignon Anderson in Thanhouser's *David Copperfield*.

"I started at seventy-five dollars. That was a lot of money, too, in those days. Mr. Thanhouser was wonderful; he was wonderful to me. Then I was raised to one hundred, and from then on, every so often, I'd get a small raise. I finished at three hundred when I left there."

Writing in *Photoplay* (November 1913), Harriet Holmes noted, "Mignon Anderson is the tiniest and dearest little mite of a girl you ever saw. She is scarcely five feet tall and weighs less than a hundred pounds. But with all her 'tiny-ness' she is one of Thanhouser's most valued leading ladies."

Mignon Anderson certainly was a valued member of the company. Among the dozens and dozens of films in which she appeared were *The Merchant of Venice* (released July 26, 1912) with William J. Bowman, Florence La Badie, and William Russell; *A Girl of the Sea* (released June 1, 1915) with Harry Benham, and *John T. Rocks and the Flivver* (released October 17, 1915) with John Holden and George M. Maslo.

Her most famous Thanhouser film, and one of her few film performances that has survived through to the present, is *The Mill on the Floss*,

Mignon Anderson and Ed Coxen in *Mountain Madness*, directed by Lloyd Carleton, produced by Republic, and released by Selznick in 1920.

directed by James Cruze, and released, through Mutual, on December 16, 1915. It was Thanhouser productions such as this that caused *Moving Picture World* to comment that "The Thanhouser products show dignity of conception and execution."

Mignon was a member of Thanhouser's "Middle Western Company," which each winter journeyed to Chicago, and also included Harry Benham, Ethyle Cooke, Leland Benham, and Frank Urson, together with cameraman William Zollinger and director T. N. Heffron.

In 1916 Mignon married fellow Thanhouser player Morris Foster, and later that year—in March, she and he left Thanhouser to join Ivan Productions. Her first film for her new company was *The City of Illusion,* directed by Ivan Abramson, owner of the concern that bore his name. Her stay with Ivan was brief, and in January 1917, Mignon Anderson signed a contract with Universal.

She worked for many directors at Universal during that first year, including Lois Weber (*Even as You and I*), Rupert Julian (*The Circus of Life*), Charles Swickard (*The Phantom's Secret*), and Ruth Ann Baldwin (*A Wife on Trial*). From 1918 onward, Mignon Anderson free-lanced; her last film, *Kisses,* was released by Metro in 1922.

All of the members of the Thanhouser Company have long since passed away; only "fillet mignon," as James Cruze nicknamed her, remains—a true pioneer of the cinema.

2

Hobart Bosworth

Hobart Bosworth was the dean of the movie industry. His film career spanned over thirty years, from 1909 to 1942. He was a distinguished actor, both in appearance and in performance, and above all, he was a gentleman. Some might say he was the last gentleman in the film industry. The cinema should be eternally grateful for the dignity that he gave to a brash, new form of entertainment.

Born in Marietta, Ohio, on August 11, 1867, the son of a Civil War sea captain, Hobart Van Zandt Bosworth ran away to sea at the age of twelve. Some years later, he found himself in San Francisco, and there made his stage debut as a super at the California Theatre in June 1881. Two months later, in August of the same year, he became a member of Augustin Daly's Stock Company.

He rose to prominence in the theatrical profession, appearing with such leading ladies as Julia Marlowe, Mrs. Fiske, Henrietta Crosman, and Amelia Bingham. In 1905 he became stage director at the Belasco Stock Company in Los Angeles, a position from which he resigned in 1909 due to ill health.

To recount Hobart Bosworth's career from this year onwards, I would like to quote at some con-

siderable length from his article, "The Picture Forty-Niners," published in the December 1915 issue of *Photoplay:*

"In May 1909, Francis Boggs, director of the Selig Polyscope company, brought the first motion picture aggregation to Los Angeles. Boggs — who was shot and killed by an insane Japanese gardener three years ago — was the real father of the moving picture industry on the coast. He opened a small temporary studio on Olive street near Eighth, almost in the heart of the business district. At that time the Turkish trouble was at its height, and Boggs, always up to date, wanted to put on a film having some special bearing on the Turkish affair. He offered me the leading part.

"I was heartily indignant and talked about my Augustin Daly traditions, but he assured me that it was a perfectly honest and legitimate way to make a living, and promised that my name would not be used in any connection with the production.

"It was called *In the Power of the Sultan* [released June 17, 1909, and also known as *In the Sultan's Power*], one reel in length, and required two days in the making.

"It was the pioneer picture in the west. Up to that time no picture had ever been produced west

Francis Boggs, Hobart Bosworth's first director at Selig.

of the Rocky Mountains. In that drama, Stella Adams, now with the Universal, played the lead and Betty Harte the juvenile lead. Tom Santschi, still with Selig as director and actor, was in the cast and was also the general utility man of the studio; James McGee was the business manager, and the other members of the little company were Frank Montgomery, who has since won renown as a director of Indian plays, and Ed Vivian, who was drowned at Redondo Beach several years ago. James Crosby, now chief of the Universal laboratory, was the cameraman.

"The plant was a vacant lot with an old building on it that served as a dressing room. I will never forget my first visit to it. My heart sank into my boots when I viewed the frightful disorder of the place. The stage was covered with carpets and debris, and, viewing my ill-concealed repugnance, Boggs said: 'Never mind the floor, we will only cut to your knees, the rest won't show.'

"That first scene was a shocking experience. I

had been accustomed to rapid fire stock production, one play a week, and it was inconceivable that sets could be got up so quickly and used so little. None was used more than two days, the average time consumed in making a reel, and while it was being done, they were preparing the scenario for the next production.

"After that first picture, Boggs made a trip to the Yosemite and Mount Shasta, returning in the fall and locating a little hall at Edendale on the northwestern edge of Los Angeles. This little green hall is now a part of the dressing rooms of the big Selig plant at Edendale.

"Boggs wrote me at San Diego, where I was fixing up a bad lung [Bosworth almost died of tuberculosis], and asked me to join his company permanently. The proposition became attractive, as I considered that it afforded me, apparently, my one last opportunity to do theatrical work. It was also open air work, and the scenes were never longer than 50 or 60 seconds in duration, with long rests between. The engagement would be for a year of 52 weeks at the usual salary of the stock leading man.

"The first picture at the Edendale studio was *The Roman,* a sort of Virginius drama. I remember the great joy I felt at that time—which still remains—at seeing the beautiful color scheme of gorgeous costumes against natural scenery.

"While making *The Roman,* Boggs thought it would be economy to get another story out of the costumes and scenery, so, although I almost died of fright at the task, I evolved my first story, around a given number of actors, scenes and props.

"Boggs worked with the tools he had in hand, but always for the betterment of the film, photographically, scenically and as regards cast.

"Within a very few weeks after I joined Boggs, I was directing and writing my own pictures, so that of the output of the Selig studio up to the time I left it, I had written 112 scenarios and I had directed 84 out of the 140 in which I appeared. I was by no means the first legitimate actor to enter the film field, but I at least was one of the earliest, and except Charles Kent, I do not know anyone in the work at that time who had achieved the same place on the legitimate stage that I had. I do know that I was almost the first—perhaps the very first—to do physical stunts that were then so necessary in putting on reel dramas."

In August 1913, Hobart Bosworth entered into an agreement with H.T. Rudisill and Frank A. Garbutt to form a new company, Bosworth Incorporated, to produce pictures based upon the stories of Jack London. "I felt that I had seized the psychological moment in putting the London long reel stories upon a market composed of so many battling elements, that someone had to buy my production on the chance that it might be good. If it was good, I had succeeded, if I failed I had at least shown my mettle, and my only philosophy in life is the rule of the survival of the fittest."

The first London story to be filmed was *The Sea Wolf,* a seven-reel feature, in which Bosworth played Wolf Larsen, supported by Herbert Rawlinson and Viola Barry. Of the production, W. Stephen Bush in *The Moving Picture World* (November 1, 1913) wrote: "It is a first effort and it is creditable and gives promise of splendid things in the future, but it is not an unqualified success. The process of adaptation must be a process of elimination, too, and the tendency even in such a picturesque tale, so rich in episode, must be toward simplifying and strengthening the action. In these requirements the present production has not reached perfection, but I am glad to add that everywhere the spectator meets glorious pictures and the subtle touch of the London variety of genius."

Of Bosworth's performance, Bush continued, "Mr. Bosworth had the physique and the artistic size required by the part, though in the characterization he was not quite as strong as in the 'straight' acting. He seemed in the early part of the story not quite certain of his ground, but as the action advanced to the great dramatic moments he electrified the audience by his masterly portrayals. He does not always succeed in expressing a mood, but a passion he can express according to Shakespeare."

During 1914, Bosworth filmed several other Jack London stories: *Burning Daylight, John Barleycorn, Martin Eden, An Odyssey of the North,* and *The Valley of the Moon.* He also filmed stories by other writers, and, most importantly, hired Lois Weber as a director—*It's No Laughing Matter, Hypocrites,* and others—and set her out on a career as the silent cinema's most famous woman director.

Bosworth Incorporated went out of existence in 1915, and Hobart Bosworth joined Universal as a leading man. One of his first Universal releases was *Tainted Money,* directed by Ulysses Davis. "For the first time in his long and varied career before the motion picture camera Hobart Bosworth plays the part of a ruffian," noted *Moving Picture World* (October 30, 1915). "He has pictured many types of western men, but he has never been known to side in with a bunch of gangsters, or to be the leader of a notorious gang. In fact, it has always been his lot to be pitted against such machinations, but in *Tainted Money* Mr. Bosworth is a sure-enough leader of bad men. And he does dirty political jobs and gets in jail for it — actually serves time — the same as all other bad men who do those pretty little things before the camera, so it goes without saying that Hobart Bosworth is as bad a bad man as he is a good good man when he plays that part."

1916 saw Bosworth under contract to Lasky as both leading man and director/writer. (Interestingly, Bosworth, Lasky, Zukor, and others had earlier combined to create Paramount Pictures.) One of Bosworth's most important roles at Lasky was as General La Hire opposite Geraldine Farrar in *Joan the Woman,* which opened at New York's 44th Street Theatre on December 25, 1916. Of the production the *New York Dramatic Mirror* (December 30, 1916) wrote, "Terrible in its realism, magnificent in its investiture, costuming and direction; acted throughout with perfect art." *Exhibitors' Trade Review* (January 6, 1917) commented "Hobart Bosworth made a splendid General La Hire."

From 1916 onward, Bosworth settled down to being an above-average leading man, starring in *Oliver Twist* (1916), *The Little American* (1917), *Behind the Door* (1919) and *A Thousand to One* (1920), among many, many others.

In 1921, Bosworth tried to return to production, and created Hobart Bosworth Productions to film *Blind Hearts* and *The Sea Lion.* Both films were directed by his old friend, Rowland V. Lee — responsible for *A Thousand to One* — and starred Bosworth himself, with Madge Bellamy as his leading lady in *Blind Hearts* and Bessie Love in *The Sea Lion.* The two productions showed Bosworth's love for outdoor life and adventure, as evidenced by his earlier filming of Jack London stories, but neither was successful.

Bosworth continued to act extensively in films for the next two decades, usually in leading

Hobart Bosworth and Geraldine Farrar in *Joan the Woman*. "Joan tells La Hire to outfit her brother, Pierre, and Gaspard to fight for her standard."

Jane Novak and Hobart Bosworth in *Behind the Door* (1919). "So I came to you. I had no other place to go."

Hobart Bosworth prepares to take Wallace Beery
Behind the Door (1919).

Lloyd Hughes (second from left) and Hobart Bosworth
in *Below the Surface* (1920).

Hobart Bosworth, Charles "Buddy" Rogers, and Mary
Pickford in *My Best Girl* (1927).

character parts. In 1927 he played Charles
"Buddy" Roger's father in the Mary Pickford vehicle *My Best Girl*. Some years ago, I mentioned to
"Buddy" Rogers my admiration of Bosworth, and
he recalled, "I remember him so well as a young
boy. We had a bridle path in Beverly Hills, and he
had this big white stallion. My first memory of
glamor Hollywood was to see him and Valentino
— to see those two men riding."

Hobart Bosworth's last screen appearance was
in Ray Enright's 1942 production of *Sin Town*. He
died in Glendale on December 30, 1943. As the *Los
Angeles Time* commented at the time, he would
not have called it death, just "going on."

In the March 10, 1917, issue of *Moving Picture
World*, Bosworth recalled his career up to that
time: "I remember the eager joy with which I cut
out a clipping from the editorial column of the *Los
Angeles Examiner*, referring in a kindly and pat-
ronizing way to the possibilities of the motion
picture, and sent it to Mr. Selig....My thoughts

revert to the little shabby yard where began the
growth of the colossal industry here in Los
Angeles—where we made that little first one-
reeler less than ten years ago. And I think of the
wonderful studios in which I'm working. It's like a
dream! As old Justice Swallow said: 'That thou
hads't seen that, that this knight and I have seen,
Jesu! The days that we have seen!' "

Hobart Bosworth in later life with Linda Darnell.

3

Billie Rhodes

It always seems extraordinary to me how much space has been devoted to the life and film career of Mabel Normand, and why so little attention has been paid to that equally talented comedienne of the same vintage, Billie Rhodes. Perhaps it is because no scandal touched and tempered Billie's career as it did Mabel Normand's, or, perhaps, it is because too few historians have taken the time to view any of Billie Rhodes's films.

Born and educated in San Francisco, Billie Rhodes — she prefers not to give her real name — began her career on the stage, playing with the Morrison Stock Company and touring on the Orpheum Circuit in *Babes in Toyland*. Her entrance into films came about as a result of Kalem director George Melford's hearing her sing at a nightclub. Melford was impressed by her charm and personality, and, after talking things over with Billie's mother, for Billie was still a minor, signed her to a contract with the Kalem Company.

Billie's first Kalem production was the two-reel *Perils of the Sea*, featuring Carlyle Blackwell and William West, and released on September 20, 1913. This was followed by *Daughter of the Underworld*, with Paul Hurst and Carlyle Blackwell, and released on October 22, 1913; and *The Big Horn Massacre*, with Paul Hurst and Jack Hoxie, and released on December 24, 1913.

After completion of her Kalem contract, Billie Rhodes returned to singing in night clubs, and as she recalls, "It wasn't long before Al Christie caught my hand one evening when I was about to sing, and asked me to come over to the studio. He was going to form a second company."

Thus, in the summer of 1915, Billie Rhodes found herself starring in Al Christie's Nestor Comedies, photographed by Al Cawood, and released through Universal. Christie was, after Mack Sennett, the most influential comedy producer of the teens, and his Universal-controlled Nestor Company was rapidly expanding. Wrote Al Ray in *Picture Play* (October 16, 1915): "Billie Rhodes, the former Kalem leading lady, is making a great success with the Nestor Company, under the direction of Al Christie. Billie is one of our best little laugh provokers, and is making the hit of her young life at the present time."

Billie appeared in one comedy a week, co-starring with Ray Gallagher, Neal Burns, Lee Moran, and Ethel Lynn. Most of these shorts were directed by Horace Davey, and included *The Boy, the Girl, and the Auto* (January 10, 1916), *Mixed Kids* (February 7, 1916), *Putting Her Foot in It* (April 10, 1916), and *His Wooden Leg* (April 24, 1916). In addition, Billie was featured in one of the most important Christie productions of 1915 or,

25

Billie Rhodes.

for that matter, any other year, *Mrs. Plum's Pudding*, directed and written by Al Christie himself, and starring Marie Tempest, with Lee Moran and Eddie Lyons.

When Christie left Nestor in the late summer of 1916 to form his own independent comedy company he took Billie Rhodes with him, and starred her in his first independent production, *A Seminary Scandal*, featuring Stella Adams and Eddie Barry, and released on September 18, 1916. Other Christie-directed comedies from this period, in which Miss Rhodes was starred, include *A Gay*

Deceiver, released January 29, 1917, and *Black Hands and Soapsuds*, released February 17, 1917.

In April 1917, it was announced that Billie was to be starred opposite Jay Belasco in a series of "Strand" Comedies, produced under the supervision of Al Christie and released through Mutual. Of Rhodes and Belasco, *Motion Picture Classic* (April 1917) commented, "They are a mighty good-looking couple, and should prove most attractive in the bright comedies the one and only Al has made his very own." The first comedy in the series, *Her Hero*, was released on April 11, 1917.

Billie Rhodes in *Her Speedy Affair* (frame enlargement).

Billie Rhodes and Ethel Lynne in *Flypapers* (frame
enlargement).

"The Strand Comedies," announced John R. Freuler, president of Mutual, "will give the exhibitor just the class of picture which will please everyone in the audience. Utterly devoid of any element of slapstick, the Strand Comedies are filled with clean, wholesome fun. They are built around the love affairs, quarrels and adventures of young people, and depict laughable incidents of every-day life played by real human people."

By 1918 Billie Rhodes was ready for starring roles in features. *Variety* (December 28, 1917) had noted that she was "Surely well on her way to a splendid future in Filmland."

William "Smiling Billy" Parsons, himself a comedian, had begun to take an interest in Billie's career. He persuaded her to part company with Christie, and starred her in a series of Capitol Comedies, for release by Goldwyn. Parsons also starred Billie in the six-reel *The Girl of My Dreams*, released through First National. For its Los Angeles opening at Tally's Theatre in September 1918, Billie made a personal appearance and entertained the audience with patriotic songs.

More features followed, under the banner of Parson's National Film Corporation of America. Billie Rhodes created a precedent by starring in two features released in the same month, March 1919. In *Hoop-La*, she portrayed "Hoop-La Charters," a circus performer, and in *The Lamb and the Lion*, she was an orphan, "Boots." *Moving Picture World* (March 15, 1919) noted "Billie Rhodes has proved in her recent five-reel productions for the National Film Corporation that comedy-drama is her forte, and it is this type of photoplay that will be furnished her in the future. Although always a purely comedy performer before she was featured in five-reelers by the National, Miss Rhodes has since showed herself a finished actress, able to handle the most dramatic situations."

Billie Rhodes's most important feature role was as Ruth in the Salvation Army drama, *The Blue Bonnet*, released in the autumn of 1919. Billie portrayed a young girl, brought up in an atmosphere of crime, but saved through the intervention of the Salvation Army. In one sequence she was required to dress up as a boy, and so realistic was her acting and make-up that, as Billie recalls, a policeman, not believing she was part of the film company, shooting on a New York Street, asked her to move along.

The critic in *Exhibitor's Trade Review* (November 8, 1919) commented, "Billie Rhodes as the featured player gives a very sincere and most satisfactory interpretation of the role entrusted to her. Ruth is one of those 'sympathetic' characters of the stage and screen and its most exacting demand is that the actress grow in years, for Ruth is first seen as a girl of twelve. Miss Rhodes meets this obligation with telling effect and one of the features of the picture is to watch Miss Rhodes 'grow.'"

Meanwhile, on February 12, 1919, Billie Rhodes had married William Parson. Their marriage was all too brief. Parsons died in Los Angeles on September 28 of the same year. He was forty-one years old. A year later, on October 8, 1920, in San Francisco, Billie married William H. Jobelmann, a director of publicity for the Turner and Dahnken Circuit.

In October 1920, Max Roth, eastern district manager for Special Pictures Corporation, announced that Billie had been signed to star in a series of twenty-six comedies for that company. The same year saw the release of her last National feature production, *Miss Nobody,* in which Billie got mixed up with outlaws on Devil's Island. Critical reception was not entirely favorable. *Photoplay* (July 1920) commented: "The villains are not all that is bad about the picture—so are the subtitles, so is Billie when she cries close to the lens. Otherwise she is cute. The story is compelling, even though the production lacks finesse. It would not do for children's matinees."

Billie Rhodes's film career was drawing to a close. In 1922 she starred in a series of Joe Rock comedies, and in the early twenties made four independent features: *His Pajama Girl* (1921), *The Star Reporter* (1921), *Fires of Youth* (1924), and *Leave It to Gerry* (1924). She returned to the stage and night club singing.

Much like Mabel Normand, Billie Rhodes's style of comedy was considered passé by the twenties. Domestic comedy was being replaced by sophisticated comedy-drama.

Miss Rhodes now lives in retirement in North Hollywood, content in the knowledge that her films brought enjoyment to millions in their day, and that through occasional reissues by Blackhawk Films, among others, she is garnering a new generation of admirers.

Billie Rhodes and Scott Beal in *The Blue Bonnet* (1919).

Billie Rhodes in the fifties.

4

Kathlyn Williams

"Any young woman who will sit down in a bathing suit and try to convince a large and vicious lion that he is wrong must be a woman of courage and poise. And Kathlyn Williams is."

So wrote Bess Burgess in the January 1917 issue of *Photoplay* of the leading lady of the Selig Poly-scope Company. Colonel William N. Selig's company was noted for its collection of wild animals, featured in many of its releases, and its players were always expected to be ready to accept a supporting role to an elephant, a chimpanzee, or a lion. Despite such demands, Kathlyn Williams always played her parts with easy grace and the manner of a lady.

Kathlyn Williams was born in Butte, Montana, on May 31, 1888. She studied drama at Wesleyan University and at the Empire School of Acting in New York. Her first screen appearance was apparently with the Biograph Company in California, in *Gold Is Not All,* released on March 28, 1910. (The winter of 1909/1910 marked the first time that director D. W. Griffith took his company of players to California.)

Miss Williams's sojourn with the Selig Company began in the winter of 1910. She soon became

Kathlyn Williams, leading lady of the Selig Company.

Kathlyn Williams (center) as Henriette in Selig's 1911
production of *The Two Orphans*.

the leading lady of the company. Early in 1911, she
portrayed Henriette, one of the two orphans—the
other was portrayed by Winnifred Greenwood—in
the film of the same name. Based on the stage play
by Kate Claxton, *The Two Orphans* was the basis
for D. W. Griffith's *The Orphans of the Storm*,
with Lillian and Dorothy Gish as the orphans in
question. It had already been filmed once before
by Selig in 1907. Kathlyn Williams also played the
title role in the cinema's first serial, *The Adventures of Kathlyn,* the first episode of which, *The
Unwelcome Throne,* was released on December
29, 1913.

In March 1913, Miss Williams married a fellow
actor, Robert Allen. The marriage ended in divorce, and on June 2, 1916, she married another
actor, Charles Eyton. That marriage lasted until
1931, when the couple were divorced. However,
they remained close friends, and at Eyton's death
in 1941, Miss Williams inherited twenty percent of
his estate.

Kathlyn Williams starred in the Selig
Company's most famous production, *The Spoilers,* which was the opening feature at S. L.
Rothapfel's Strand Theatre in New York. Based
on the novel by Rex Beach and directed by Colin
Campbell, *The Spoilers* has since been remade
four times. *Variety* (April 17, 1914) commented,
"Kathlyn Williams looked after the Cherry Mar-
lotte character so effectively it is doubtful if any
other actress could have improved upon the part."
(Released originally as a nine-reel feature, *The
Spoilers* was reissued in 1916 in a twelve-reel version, which included an appearance by Rex
Beach.)

Among the many dozens of Selig shorts in which
Miss Williams was featured were: *Captain Kate*
and *1861* (both 1911); *The Adopted Son, As the*

Kathlyn Williams in Episode One, "The Unwelcome Throne" of *The Adventures of Kathlyn*, released December 29, 1913.

A typical Selig publicity shot of Kathlyn Williams from *The Adventures of Kathlyn*.

A glamorized Kathlyn Williams in the twenties.

Fates Decree, and *The Brotherhood of Man* (all 1912); *A Wise Old Elephant, Woman – Past and Present, The Artist and the Brute, The Burglar Who Robbed Death,* and *A Child of the Sea* (all 1913); *A Woman Laughs, Caryl of the Mountains,* and *Chip of the Flying "U"* (all 1914); *The Rosary* (1915) and *The Ne'er Do Well* (1916).

In 1914, Kathlyn Williams wrote, directed, and starred in *The Leopard's Foundling,* released on June 29, 1914. In an interview in *Feature Movie Magazine* (April 15, 1915), Miss Williams was quoted, "Women can direct just as well as men, and in the manner of much of the planning they often have a keener artistic sense and more of an eye for detail — and often it is just one tiny thing—five feet of film maybe — that spoils a picture, for it is always the little things that go wrong that one remembers."

The end of 1916 saw the Selig Company rapidly losing ground as a major producer. Like many of its players, Kathlyn Williams decided to leave, and signed a long-term contract with Oliver Morosco's company, which released through Paramount. She soon became one of Paramount's most popular stars.

Something of Miss Williams's versatility as an actress may be perceived from her performance in the 1917 production of *The Cost of Hatred,* directed by George Melford, in which she attempted a dual role of mother and daughter. *Variety* (April 13, 1917) commented, "Miss Williams gives an exceedingly interesting performance, while

Kathlyn Williams, as Queen Isabel of Bourbon, with Wallace Beery, as King Philip IV, in *The Spanish Dancer* (1923).

The New York Dramatic Mirror (April 14, 1917) considered "Kathlyn Williams is very effective as the wife, but is hardly ingenue enough to make a satisfactory daughter."

Miss Williams starred in three features for director William C. de Mille, *The Tree of Knowledge, The Prince Chap,* and *Conrad in Quest of His Youth.* (Interestingly, *The Prince Chap,* based on a play by Edward Peple, had been filmed by Selig in 1916, but with another of the company's leading ladies, Bessie Eyton, in the role Kathlyn Williams essayed for Paramount). *Conrad in Quest of His Youth,* based on the novel by Leonard Merrick, and featuring Thomas Meighan as Conrad, is an utter delight. Conrad searches for his youth, after the First World War, and finds that life has changed, and it is impossible to restore the past. Miss Williams plays Mrs. Adaile, whom Conrad had remembered as the most beautiful woman in the world.

During 1921 Kathlyn was featured in five films with May McAvoy: *A Private Scandal, A Virginia Courtship, Morals, Everything for Sale* and *Clarence.* The same year her contract with Paramount ended, and Miss Williams free-lanced. No longer able to portray ingenues, she was ideally cast as slightly aging women, unaware that they are no longer young. In over thirty films in the twenties, Kathlyn Williams was a featured character player, some of her films being *The Spanish Dancer* (1923), *Wanderer of the Wasteland* (1924), *The Wanderer* (1926) and *Our Dancing Daughters* (1928).

She made an easy transition to sound, but preferred to work only infrequently. Among Miss Williams's talkies were *Wedding Rings* (1930), *Daddy Long Legs* (1931), *Unholy Love* (1932), and *Blood Money* (1933). Her last screen appearance was in Universal's 1935 production of *Rendezvous at Midnight,* directed by Christy Cabanne. The players, who included Ralph Bellamy and Valerie Hobson, were praised, but the film itself was not. *Film Daily* (March 26, 1935) commented, "As murder melodramas go, this one rates rather low."

One of the last photographs of Kathlyn Williams, taken in her Los Angeles apartment.

In January 1950, Kathlyn Williams was involved in a serious road accident, which resulted in her right leg being amputated. She became bitter and dispirited, but was comforted by the letters she received from many thousands of fans who still remembered her. Kathlyn Williams died on September 24, 1960, in her Los Angeles apartment.

36

PART II.

The Idols of the Teens

5
Elmer Clifton

No director could ask for better training than that of being a member of D. W. Griffith's company, just as no actor could desire more. Elmer Clifton was doubly lucky. He played juvenile leads in Griffith's two finest productions, and under the great director's aegis became a director himself.

Strangely, Clifton has received little recognition. If he is remembered at all as a director, it is by "B" western enthusiasts. In discussions of Griffith's players, his name is seldom mentioned. It is perhaps the lot of a good actor to give a performance that is unnoticed by the very nature of its perfect fusion into the film as a whole.

Elmer Clifton was born on March 15, 1890, on one of the islands in the St. Lawrence River. After schooling in Chicago, he joined a theatrical stock company there. He played with Hobart Bosworth in New York, and later joined Lewis Stone's stock company, touring California. On the New York stage, he appeared in *The Girl of the Golden West, The Brass Bottle,* and *The Deep Purple,* among others. In 1913 he again toured California this time with Richard Bennett's company.

It was on this trip to California that Clifton was approached by Hobart Bosworth and offered the leading role in Bosworth's own film production of *John Barleycorn.* Of his performance, *Moving Picture World* (July 18, 1914) wrote, "His [Clifton's] was no easy task, but he proved fully equal to what was asked of him. He enlists our sympathy from the first and skillfully sustains and stimulates it."

D. W. Griffith saw his performance in *John Barleycorn* and was so impressed that he asked Clifton to join his company. The director cast the young man in the role of Phil Stoneman in *The Birth of a Nation.* Clifton brought a unique manliness and heroic virility to the role of the eldest son of the Northern family. His love scenes with Miriam Cooper are in perfect counterpoint to the love scenes between Henry B. Walthall and Lillian Gish.

Elmer Clifton was cast in Griffith's second masterwork, *Intolerance.* This time, he portrayed a very different role, that of the Rhapsode in the Babylonian story, who dotes upon the Mountain Girl (Constance Talmadge). Again, he was perfectly at ease in a difficult characterization. Again, as in *The Birth of a Nation,* no contemporary reviewers singled out his performance for special mention.

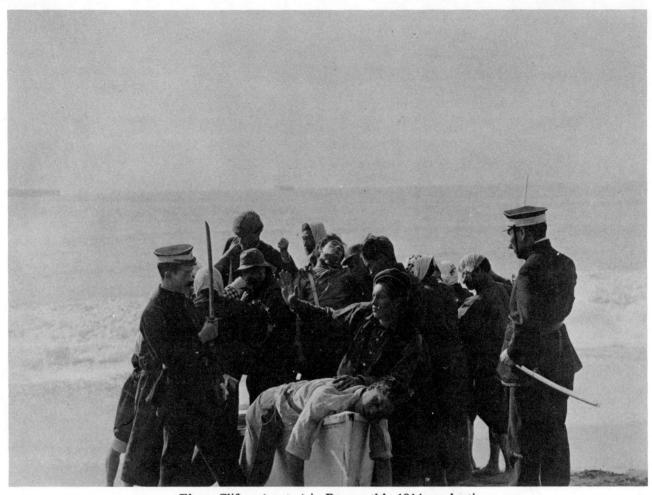

Elmer Clifton (center) in Bosworth's 1914 production of *John Barleycorn*. "The end of the Bonin Island Saki spree."

Elmer Clifton as Phil Stoneman in *The Birth of a Nation* (1915).

The very essence of masculinity. Elmer Clifton as Phil
Stoneman in *The Birth of a Nation*.

A not-at-all masculine Elmer Clifton, as the Rhapsode,
with Constance Talmadge, as the Mountain Girl, in
Intolerance (1916).

Clifton also appeared in other Griffith productions for Fine Arts, the organization with which the director was associated. Many were written by Griffith under a pseudonym; all were nominally supervised by him. Among such films were *The Sable Lorcha* (released October 17, 1915), *The Lily and the Rose* (released December 5, 1915), *The Missing Link* (released January 16, 1916, and *The Little School Ma'am* (released July 16, 1916).

D. W. Griffith obviously had a high opinion of Elmer Clifton's abilities. He used Clifton as an assistant director on both *The Birth of a Nation* and *Intolerance*. More importantly, Griffith appreciated and relied on the young man's advice. Eventually, early in 1917, Griffith allowed him to direct his first film in collaboration with Joseph Henabery. *Her Official Fathers* was released on April 8, 1917. It was five reels in length, and featured Dorothy Gish as Janice Webster, supported by Frank Bennett and Sam De Grasse.

The reviews in the trade press were fairly favorable. Commented *Variety* (April 13, 1917), "The piece is comedy of a high order, and is well worth a place on a 'big time' program." *The Moving Picture World* (April 14, 1917) thought *"Her Official Fathers* is a light and pleasing comedy, short weight in material but made very entertaining through clever handling and a fine cast, with Dotty Dimple Dorothy at her best." The response from the fan magazines was not as favorable. In a reference to the impending demise of the Fine Arts Company, Julian Johnson in *Photoplay* (June 1917) described *Her Official Fathers* as "The weak gesture of a dying giant."

Elmer Clifton directed a couple more Dorothy Gish comedies at Fine Arts, aided by a young cameraman, Karl Brown, before departing for a directorial position with Universal. During 1917 and 1918, he directed many Universal releases, including *The Midnight Man, A Stormy Knight, The Man Trap, Flirting with Death,* and *The Flash of Fate.*

In 1918 Elmer Clifton returned to Griffith's company to direct Dorothy Gish in a series of comedies that Griffith was supervising for release through Paramount-Artcraft. These Dorothy Gish comedies were immensely successful. They kept Griffith financially sound, and helped both Miss Gish and Clifton to gain a solid reputation as filmmakers.

Aside from the Gish comedies, Clifton worked very closely with Griffith during 1919 and 1920 on the production of *Way Down East.* Clifton in biographical notes has described himself as Associate Director of the film, although he receives no credit on the film itself. He most certainly shot some of the scenes on the ice, and would appear to have doubled for Richard Barthelmess, but to what extent is unclear. What is clear is that whatever Clifton's contribution to the film may have been, he carried it out with modesty and enthusiasm.

Elmer Clifton never forgot his debt to Griffith. In the June 1922 issue of *Motion Picture Magazine,* he told Gladys Hall, "It isn't a question of influence. I simply believe in Mr. Griffith's methods, because they are truths. His great points are young love and the 'run to the rescue.' They will be mine. Young love and the romance of youth, whether it be love or adventure, is the primary, the all-important thing. Who wants to see age depicted? We all know that it exists, and that it is coming to us, but it is youth we wish to watch, youth we wish to recapture, if only in a vision."

Clifton left Griffith to begin work on what was to be his finest achievement as a director, *Down to the Sea in Ships.* He spent a year working on this epic of whaling, shooting on the open sea and in New Bedford, Massachusetts. It made a star of its juvenile leading lady, Clara Bow, and was widely praised. Writing in *The Best Moving Pictures of 1922-23,* Robert E. Sherwood commented, *"Down to the Sea in Ships* stands as a fine achievement for Elmer Clifton and for the people of New Bedford. The fact that they undertook the job is commendable in itself, the fact that they made a success of it is little short of miraculous."

Never again did Elmer Clifton reach the heights of *Down to the Sea in Ships.* He signed a seven-year contract with William Fox, but directed only three features, *Six Cylinder Love* (1923), *Daughters of the Night* (1924), and *The Warrens of Virginia* (1924). In 1926, he joined Cecil B. DeMille Productions, and directed *The Wreck of the Hesperus.* By 1928, he had sunk to the depths of Tiffany-Stahl and Columbia. In the thirties, he settled down to directing westerns, usually featuring Buck Jones.

Elmer Clifton never could become a part of the studio system. He was always working on exciting, independent projects that came to naught. It was while at work on such a project that he suffered a thrombosis of the brain, and died on October 15, 1949.

Down to the Sea in Ships, premiered at the Olympia Theatre, New Bedford, on September 25, 1922. "They that go down to the sea in ships, that do business on the great waters. These see the works of the Lord and his wonders of the deep." — Psalm 107.

Cameraman Alexander G. Penrod, director Elmer Clifton with stars Raymond McKee and Marguerite Courtot. The two players fell in love and were married while the film was in production.

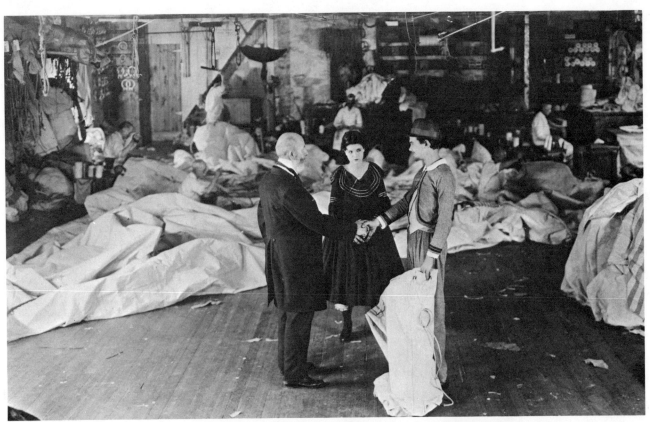

Clara Bow, as "Dot" Morgan, became a star as a result
of her performance in *Down to the Sea in Ships*.

"The rural vista of this old country road in the purlieus of New Bedford shows the quaintness of the golden days of whaling when the oxen of the countryside hauled the newly made whale boats to the docks to be shipped on the square-rigged whalers sailing from the port."— Elmer Clifton.

6
Olga Petrova

"*It is always depressing* to contemplate how many films of great actresses and actors have been lost. In the cases of many players from the silent era, few, if any, of their films have survived. Olga Petrova was highly regarded between 1914 and 1920 as one of the cinema's finest dramatic actresses, yet at the time of writing only one of her films is known to have survived (in the collection of George Eastman House).

Olga Petrova was a true noblewoman among the ranks of silent screen actresses. Constance Severance in *Photoplay* (October 1916) wrote of her: "She is a patrician of the voiceless stage. Count upon your fingers—and you won't need many —the actresses in pictures or out, whom you can imagine in the environment of a royal court, taking their places with the utmost dignity and unconscious ease among princesses of the blood. What name comes to mind so instantly as that of Petrova? Whether obeying the mandates of a director, or daintily engaged in making Lobster Newberg, she never loses that poise and elegance of manner, because she never assumes it. It is part of her. One would as soon write her a 'mash note' as invite the President to dine at Childs.''

Louis Willoughby's favorite photograph of his wife, Olga Petrova.

PETROVA

PICTURES

Madame Petrova (center) in *The Black Butterfly* (1916).
"In the Apache Den, Sonia meets Alan."

Aside from her acting abilities, Madame Petrova was quite a remarkable woman. At a time when a woman was definitely subordinate to a man, she was liberated—not only in terms of her independence and determination to take care of herself, but also in the roles that she portrayed on the screen. No sweet young ingenue or devoted heroine for Petrova. Her characters were women of ability with minds of their own and personalities of their own. For example, in her 1918 feature *The Light Within,* she portrayed a doctor of bacteriology, who discovers a cure for meningitis and anthrax.

In the September 1918 issue of *Motion Picture Classic,* she told Frederick James Smith, "I do want to bring a message to women—a message of encouragement. The only women I want to play are women who *do* things. I want to encourage women to do things—to take their rightful place in life." If anything was Petrova's philosophy of life, it was this.

Petrova's fight for women's rights did not take place purely in the medium of the film. While acting on the screen she was writing verse, such as "Thus Speaks Woman," in which she proclaimed:

Madame Petrova as vaudeville fans saw her.

Clarion clear it shreiks and howls
From world to world. Ave *Woman Reigns.*

Her whole life was a struggle for independence for herself and for her sex. Much of this struggle is recorded in her autobiography, *Butter with My Bread,* published by Bobbs-Merrill in 1941. In it, she tells of her early life in England, and of her fight to break free of her tyrannical father, and to gain independence. As Madame Petrova, herself, expressed it to me in a letter, her autobiography is "a tale of my struggle as a female child to break away from that life, a struggle to obtain by devious means—the screen happening to be one of them—a home, bread, and butter of my own."

Through hard work and talent, Olga Petrova became a prominent British stage actress. She was brought to the States by William Harris and Jesse Lasky, who wished to feature her in a production of the Follies Bergere, which they planned to open in New York. The show failed, but Petrova stayed on, and put together a vaudeville act that was a terrific success. This is what *Variety* (April 6, 1912) thought of her performance after seeing it at

New York's Fifth Avenue Theatre: "After all, there may be something in management and stage direction. During the short but tempestuous reign of the Follies Bergere music hall in the metropolis, there appeared a tall, lithe young woman calling herself Petrova, doing songs, etc., with a suspiciously strong foreign accent. She failed to 'make good' there and was later sent on a tour of the vaudeville houses, where she encountered a similar fate. The woman was clever but overburdened with affectation. Since Jesse Lasky has quit playing the impresario game and settled down to business, he has taken Miss Petrova in hand and coached her until she now has one of the cleverest, classiest and most attractive of 'single turns.' She opens with a double-voiced rendition of 'My Hero,' followed by 'Expressions,' a semi-recitative number, in which she imitates animals cleverly and amusingly. This in turn is succeeded by an emotion-dramatic scene from *Sapho.* For an encore she sings a French translation of 'Oh, You Beautiful Doll.' It is not so much what Miss Petrova does, but the 'way she does it.' And inciden-

Madame Petrova in the gown that she wore in her stage success, *The White Peacock*. Photograph by Tom Fulbright.

Madame Petrova in *The Scarlet Woman* (1916).

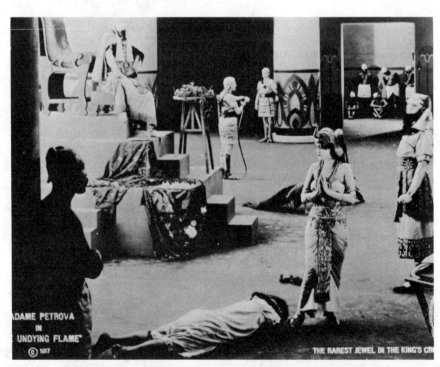

Madame Petrova loved working with director Maurice
Tourneur, and calls attention to the detail and composi-
tion in this still from *The Undying Flame* (1917).

tally her (to us) original manner of 'bowing' after each number was sufficient to mark her with the stamp of originality. Monday night she was easily the applause hit of a bill replete with excellent acts."

Early in 1913, Petrova was starred in Monkton Hoffe's play *Panthea*. She was an immediate success. While playing with the play in Chicago, on July 11, 1914, she was offered a contract to appear in films. As she recalled to Lynde Denig (*Moving Picture World,* July 24, 1915), "I was playing in *Panthea* in Chicago without the first thought of photoplay work, when it seemed wise to accept an offer that did not interfere with my engagement. The first picture was a success and there was nothing to prevent my signing a contract for others. Merely considered from the standpoint of publicity, an actress gains more from being starred in pictures shown throughout the country than could be purchased for $50,000 expended in advertising. Acting in pictures is distinctly worthwhile."

Petrova's first film, *The Tigress,* was directed by the cinema's first woman director, Madame Alice Guy Blaché. Four reels in length, it was produced by Popular Plays and Players, and re-leased by Alco, a subsidiary of Metro. *The Tigress* was well received. *Variety* (December 25, 1914) commented, "The feature has a plentitude of thrills, capital acting throughout, particularly on the part of Mme. Petrova, who is disclosed as a cinema artist of a good deal of power, and finally a quantity of highly effective studio work."

In April 1915, Petrova signed a two-year contract with Popular Plays and Players, to appear in sixteen films. The first under this contract was again directed by Madame Blaché, and was titled *The Heart of a Painted Woman.* Comparison with Petrova's work on the stage was bound to happen. Although Petrova herself obviously preferred the stage, *Variety* (April 23, 1915), reviewing *The Heart of a Painted Woman,* considered, "Miss Petrova gives a much better performance on the screen than she has ever given on the stage."

During the spring of 1917, representatives of Famous Players-Lasky approached Madame Petrova, and invited her to sign a contract with that company. With the promise of the privilege of approving the stories, technicians, and cast, Petrova signed.

Her first Famous Players release was *The Undying Flame,* directed by one of the great names of

Madame Petrova in *The Exile* (1917), another of her productions with Maurice Tourneur.

the cinema, Maurice Tourneur. In her autobiography, Petrova recalled: "Looking back now on the weeks spent in the filming of that picture, I see them as an oasis in the desert of my cinema experiences. The film itself, apart from any share I had in it, was one that I could view with little criticism, no embarrassment and a great deal of aesthetic pleasure. As a manager Mr. Lasky was considerate, indulgent and sensitive. Mr. Tourneur was all and more than I had expected as a director. For the first time since I had faced a camera lens. I could relax from the tension of worry, fear and distrust, and place myself without question under the guidance of a man, who I knew, *knew;* a man who knew that he knew; a man of culture and imagination."

If the film could be criticized, it was because of Petrova's apparent coldness in her acting. Julian Johnson, writing in *Photoplay* (August 1917), picked up this point, and commented, "If Olga

Petrova had put her corsets back in the trunk, and had, for a few minutes, stood close enough to a stove to thaw out, *The Undying Flame* would have been a very artistic production. She is eternal ice."

Under her Lasky contract, Olga Petrova starred in two more films—*Exile* and *The Law of the Land*—both directed by Tourneur, and both with Wyndham Standing as her leading man. Both features received favorable reviews. Of *Exile, The New York Dramatic Mirror* wrote, "Olga Petrova as the unhappy wife of Perez [Wyndham Standing] played with her usual ability and presented a convincing picture in her attempts to remain true to her marriage vows."

On August 1, 1917, Petrova signed her last film contract, this time with Frederick L. Collins. The company was to be known as the Petrova Picture Company, and was to release through the recently formed First National. Some five features were

Madame Petrova with her second husband, actor Louis Willoughby.

produced, the first being *Daughter of Destiny,* directed by George Irving. The best of the group was possibly *The Light Within,* directed by Larry Trimble.

After completion of *The Panther Woman,* directed by Ralph Ince, and based on the popular novel *Patience Sparhawk,* by Gertrude Atherton, Petrova decided to call it a day as far as her film career was concerned. She had suffered a nervous breakdown, and there were problems regarding the release of her films through First National.

Petrova became increasingly involved in writing, producing verse, interviews, feature articles, plays, and novels. Her 1922 play, *Hurricane,* advocated birth control, while in *What Do We Know?,* she gave a serious look at spiritualism. After the latter closed in 1919, Petrova decided she had sufficiently buttered her bread, and retired from professional life.

Now living in Florida, Madame Olga Petrova can look back on a life spent in pioneering in many fields: women's rights, the screen, and the stage. She dismisses any claim to greatness with the comment, "What is little? What is great? Let me put it this way I did achieve what I set out as a child to get, my own bread, my own butter, my own house in which to enjoy it. That—to me—is the height of what I will accept and acknowledge as greatness."

A recent portrait of the still-vivacious Madame Olga Petrova.

7

Henry B. Walthall

To few actors and actresses is given the opportunity to appear in a film masterpiece. Few players when given that opportunity have the greatness—and the humility—to portray the role adequately. From the silent era, one recalls only two: Mae Marsh in *Intolerance,* and Henry B. Walthall in *The Birth of a Nation.*

For all time, Henry B. Walthall will be the "little colonel" of *The Birth of a Nation.* As Lillian Gish wrote in her autobiography, " 'Wally,' as he was affectionately called, was everything in life that his 'little colonel' was on the screen, dear, patient, lovable." All of Walthall's films up to *The Birth of a Nation* might be described as training for that one role, and nothing that he did later could hope to compare with it.

Henry Walthall was born on March 16 or 17, 1878, on a farm near Columbiana, Shelby County, Alabama, he was one of eleven brothers. At his father's suggestion, he studied law in Birmingham, Alabama, but quit before graduating to fight, as a private, in the Spanish-American War. After that war, rather than return to law school, Walthall decided to try the stage.

In 1901 he came to New York, and made his debut there as an extra in *Secret Service,* with

Henry V. Donnelly's Murray Hill Theater stock company. After this engagement, he joined a stock company in Providence, Rhode Island. Walthall then toured with various companies: he played Captain Clay Randolph in Edward McWade's Civil War drama, *Winchester,* and for three seasons he portrayed Steve Danbury in Lottie Blair Parker's *Under Southern Skies.*

Around 1905 Henry B. Walthall joined the Broadway company of Henry Miller and Margaret Anglin, appearing with them in *The Great Divide,* among others, for four seasons. In the summer of 1909, Walthall sought out his old friend, James Kirkwood, and as he recalled in the August 1915 issue of *Photoplay.* "I received an awful shock at the Kirkwood home. Mrs. Jim told me that her husband was working in the movies. I was horrified. Then I determined to rescue him. I asked where he was working and she said he had gone to Greenwich, Conn., for the day to take a scene. She told me where I could find him the next day, at the Biograph studio.

"Having decided to rescue Jim from the clutches of the despised movies I went to the Biograph the next day. My worst fears were realized. Jim was in convicts' stripes. He seemed insensible

56

Henry B. Walthall, an early portrait.

to the shame of the situation. I blushed for him but no one noticed it. They were all too busy or too well satisfied with themselves. While they were putting up a set, Kirkwood introduced me to Griffith. I had never heard of him, but he had seen me in *Under Southern Skies* and *The Great Divide*.

" 'You are just the man I want,' said Griffith. 'Just the right type. Get on these old clothes, take this shovel and come on out in the street. There's a nice little sewer trench out there that will just fit you and bye-and-bye your sweet little daughter will bring papa his lunch.' "

Walthall's screen debut was in *A Convict's Sacrifice*, released on July 26, 1909. Walthall did, as it turned out, like film work—not to mention the regular income that it offered—and after a ten-weeks' engagement with Henry Miller's company in London, he became a permanent member of the Biograph stock company.

He remained a year with Biograph, and then joined Reliance. From Reliance, Walthall went to the Pathé Company for six months, and then back to Reliance. Walthall apparently rejoined Griffith while in California in the spring of 1912, and his first film after his return to Biograph would appear to be *Home Folks,* released on June 6, 1912.

In the spring of 1913, Griffith began shooting *Judith of Bethulia* in California. For his two principal players, he chose Blanche Sweet to portray the widow Judith, and Henry B. Walthall, to play Holofernes. There was some question as to whether the short—he was only five feet six inches—Walthall had the stature of Holofernes, but, as Blanche Sweet recalls, Griffith's reply was always, "Wally will play it big."

Of Griffith's relationship to Walthall, Miss Sweet remembers: "He loved Wally. He thought he was a fine actor, and he never really had much

Josephine Crowell and Henry B. Walthall in *Home Sweet Home* (1914).

to say about Wally's acting. He showed him very little. He just said, 'Well, here's the situation,' this that and the other, or 'a little less Wally,' or 'a little more Wally.' He respected and depended upon Wally as an actor.''

Judith of Bethulia was the last production Griffith was to direct for Biograph. In the summer of 1913 he went to Reliance-Majestic, taking with him most of his players, including Walthall, after the actor had appeared in a number of non-Griffith Biographs. *Judith* was released in the States on March 7, 1914; it had already been seen in Europe the previous year.

The first Griffith-directed Reliance-Majestic production in which Walthall appeared was *Home, Sweet Home.* The film comprises three separate stories, describing how the sentiment in John Howard Payne's song affected to the better the lives of various individuals. Walthall portrayed composer Payne in the prologue and epilogue. Of the feature, which opened at Clune's Auditorium, Los Angeles, on May 4, 1914, Harry Aitken proudly commented (in *Reel Life,* May 4, 1914), ''This will be the first great all-star production for the film and will show more effectively than anything else I can imagine the size and strength of Mr. Griffith's great company in Los Angeles.''

Walthall next worked for Griffith in *The Avenging Conscience,* portraying the antihero of the film, loosely based on various writings of Edgar Allan Poe. Commented the *New York Dramatic Mirror* (August 12, 1914): ''Henry B. Walthall is convincing in a difficult role; Blanche Sweet at times suggests the ethereal Annabel Lee that Poe must have imagined, and Spottiswoode Aiken is a wise choice for the part of the uncle. Needless to say other players were selected with care and sufficiently rehearsed in the Griffith method of acting. There is none better.''

With his next Griffith production, *The Birth of a Nation,* and his role as the ''little colonel,'' Henry B. Walthall achieved screen immortality. ''The Edwin Booth of the Screen,'' one critic dubbed him.

However, by the time *The Birth of a Nation* was ready for a New York opening in March of 1915, Walthall had left Griffith's company, and signed a contract to become leading man, at a salary of two hundred fifty dollars a week, with the Balboa Amusement Company, which released its produc-

tions through Pathé. His stay with Balboa was short, he became involved in litigation with the studio, and returned to Griffith.

He was not to stay for long. In the late spring of 1915, Walthall and his wife, Mary Charleson signed a contract with Essanay. Walthall's first production for the Chicago-based company was *Temper,* released on July 13, 1915.

Walthall was to return to Griffith's direction twice again: To portray Sir Roger Brighton in *The Great Love* (1918) and for the minor role of Colonel Marshall in *Abraham Lincoln* (1930). Interestingly, in 1926, Frederick James Smith asked Griffith to name the greatest actor he had directed. ''He thought for a while. 'Arthur Johnson, I guess,' he said. 'Yes, Arthur Johnson. Henry B. Walthall was excellent in romantic roles. Perhaps a little too florid...But Johnson was matchless in everything—modern, romantic, comedy....' ''

In May of 1917, Walthall severed his connections with the Essanay Company. A report in *Variety* (May 18, 1917) noted, ''The services of Henry B. Walthall have been offered around New York the past few days at $2,500 a week.'' Henry B. Walthall appeared to have reached an impasse. The climax in his acting career had been his performance in *The Birth of a Nation.* He could never equal that performance again; everything in the future was to be an anticlimax.

He formed an independent company, to release through Paralta. ''To become the head of my own producing company is the realization of a dream I have cherished for many years,'' he remarked to *Photo-Play Journal* (December 1917). The first release of his new company, *His Robe of Honor,* is chiefly of interest because of its director, Rex Ingram. Walthall followed this with *Humdrum Brown,* also directed by Ingram, and with *With Hoops of Steel,* in which Walthall claimed to play a cowboy for the first time.

After returning to the stage in 1918, to appear at New York's Criterion Theatre in *The Awakening,* Walthall signed a contract with the National Film Corporation, recently taken over by the newly formed Robertson-Cole Company. (Robertson Cole were at that time preparing for release *And a Still Small Voice,* another Walthall independent production.)

Walthall's film career was declining rapidly. As John Griggs noted in his tribute to Walthall in the March 1952 issue of *Films in Review,* ''In 1922,

Henry B. Walthall in his most famous role as the Little Colonel in *The Birth of a Nation* (1915).

with the rise of Wallace Reid and Rudolph Valentino, Walthall's vogue was considered over and Hollywood wrote him off as a top star. He took to the road on the Orpheum Circuit in a dramatic sketch, 'The Unknown Soldier.'''

However, Walthall was still in demand for major character roles and the occasional lead. Between 1920 and 1930, he was featured in forty-eight films, including Tod Browning's *Road to Mandalay* (1926) and *London after Midnight* (1927) and Victor Seastrom's *The Scarlet Letter* (1927).

With the coming of sound, Henry B. Walthall, with his stage background, found himself much in demand, particularly when a film called for a slightly dotty professor or scientist. In the 1932 *Chandu the Magician,* he portrayed that extraordinary contradiction in terms, a humanitarian who invents a death ray. In the 1935 *Dante's Inferno,* he was the sideshow operator at a fairground, offering his patrons a glimpse of hell. Tod Browning's 1936 production of *The Devil Doll* had Walthall proclaiming, ''You think I'm mad. The world would too, if it knew what I was going to do.'' Mad or sane, one thing was certain, Henry B. Walthall would always add dignity to a role, however silly that role might be.

In one sound film, Walthall almost achieved the

Marceline Day and Henry B. Walthall in *London after Midnight* (1927).

Lionel Barrymore and Henry B. Walthall in *The Devil Doll* (1936).

greatness of his role in *The Birth of a Nation.* That film was John Ford's 1934 production of *Judge Priest,* in the final reel of which Walthall, as the Rev. Ashby Brand, recalls the last struggles of the Confederacy in the Civil War. In the final scene, as he marches beside Will Rogers and the proudly held Confederate flag, it is almost as if the "little colonel" were reborn.

Henry B. Walthall was being considered for the role of the High Lama in Frank Capra's *Lost Horizon,* but he died, on June 17, 1936, before he could be tested for the part.

D. W. Griffith was told of the actor's death the following day, when he returned to Los Angeles from Texas. He spoke the following words, for the *Los Angeles Times* which serve as a fitting epitaph to Walthall. "I knew nothing about Mr. Walthall's death until I got off the train tonight.

"You can imagine the shock to me. I had been to the Texas Centennial in Dallas to make a dedicatory address at the unveiling of the Robert E. Lee monument in Lee Park. While there as a guest of the Daughters of the Confederacy, I was questioned about whether I ever intended to remake *The Birth of a Nation* as a talking picture.

"I had never seriously considered doing so, but if I ever had, there is no chance of doing it now, for I can never imagine any man taking the place of

Henry B. Walthall, with Will Rogers, in his finest talkie role as the Reverend Ashby Brand in *Judge Priest* (1934).

Henry B. Walthall in that picture. His death is reason enough to end all suggestions that the picture ever be remade.

"I don't know whether you could call him a great actor, but of this I am certain—he had a great soul.

"It is given perhaps to many to have great souls; it is given to only a few to be able to express that soul to the entire world by means of an expressive face and body, as Henry Walthall did in *The Birth of a Nation*.

"Of course, the world doesn't know and doesn't bother much about that sort of thing, but he had a poet's imagination and a beautiful face that could express the soul and imagination he possessed.

"He was a gentleman, and, as Hollywood puts it, 'a sweet guy.'"

PART III.

The Stars of the Twenties

8

Priscilla Bonner

Washington-born Priscilla Bonner's performances as the innocent heroine of many silent
films have never been fully appreciated. She
began her screen career playing opposite Charles
Ray in Thomas Ince's production of *Homer
Comes Home* in 1920, and retired almost ten years
later in 1929. Miss Bonner was featured in over
thirty films, but is now remembered, perhaps, for
only one, *The Strong Man,* in which she portrayed
the blind girl who loves, and is loved by, Harry
Langdon. Her sister, Marjorie (the widow of Malcolm Lowry), was also a Hollywood actress during the twenties, and the two girls appeared together in the 1927 Columbia production of *Paying
the Price.* The following interview was recorded at
Miss Bonner's Beverly Hills apartment.

"I was never on the stage. Very briefly, I was
going to school in Washington, and studying dancing. I loved to dance. One day, a young man came
to the school, he was a small man, and he was very
dark, and he was looking for a dancing partner. So
all of the senior girls were brought out to dance for
him, plus me. I was a very small girl, and I had
naturally blonde hair, and I was a very good
dancer. He chose me! I was wildly excited, and I
wrote to my mother and father back where they

Priscilla Bonner.

were living, and said he was on the Orpheum Circuit, he had offered me this contract, and I wanted to go and become a professional dancer. Here I was a little innocent young thing, and a private school! There was a long distance call—back in those days long distance calls were not like they are now; it was momentous, someone had to be dead—mother is leaving in the morning. And mother arrived, and that was the end of that.

"But it gave me something I had never had before. I wanted to be a performer. One thing led to another, and finally they allowed me to come out here. Well, it was amazing. I just seemed to go from one thing to the other.

"I went out to Metro, and there was a man there, Mr. Robertson—his son is a star now, Cliff Robertson—who was the casting director, and I walked into his office. Of course, I was very nicely dressed, but as a very young girl would be, I was just out of boarding school. So I walked in, and said I wanted to see Mr. Robertson. They said what about, and I said I'd come out here to go in pictures. Everybody was so surprised, they took me in. Mr. Robertson said, 'What's your name' I told him, Priscilla Bonner—that's my real name. He said, 'Why are you coming to see me?' So, I said, 'Well, I came out here to go in pictures,' and he said, 'What experience have you had?' And I said, 'Oh, I haven't had any experience, but I expect you to give me some.' I'll tell you what he

Will Rogers and Priscilla Bonner in *Honest Hutch* (1920).

Bessie Love and Priscilla Bonner in *Purple Dawn* (1923).

William Boyd, Priscilla Bonner, and Ronald Colman in
Tarnish (1924).

said. He leaned back in his chair, and said, 'Jesus Christ.'

"Of course, I wasn't used to such language, and I was shocked, but the end of thing was he gave me some extra work. Now, I didn't know I was an extra, and I didn't know I was to be paid, so I worked for four or five days, and I never collected any money. I was the original freshman. I didn't know anything!

"Then, I decided I didn't like what I was doing out at that studio, and I decided I would like to have something a little better. I went down to the Ince studio, where Charles Ray was working. Again, I said I was down here to go into pictures and they saw me as the type of girl they wanted. So I ended up playing the lead with Charles Ray in *Homer Comes Home* [1920]. Of course, I was pretty bad in the picture, except sweet, young, fresh. I went down to Robinson's and bought all my clothes. I think I had eight or ten changes, which the studio would have paid for, but nobody told me, so I went and bought them. They let me when they found out how stupid I was.

"When I got through with that picture, I went out to Metro again, and I think I must have been a bit of a joke about that time, because they let me in right away. Mr. Robertson said, 'Hello, how are you?' I said, 'I'm just fine now, and I'm playing leads. I've just finished playing a lead with Charles Ray.' And again he leaned back in his chair and said, 'Jesus Christ.'

"As a result, I ended up playing leads with Jack Pickford. It was unbelievable. It just went on. I had no fear because I had been gently raised in a home of protection. I wasn't afraid of anything or anybody. I had no fear of not getting work because I had come all this way to get it. Also, my innocence protected me, as it always does, you know.

"Jack Pickford was marvelous to me. He treated me like a little sister, and protected and watched over me. The whole company went up to San Francisco, and they all went on a Chinatown binge, but I wasn't taken. I was left home and carefully protected. I wasn't allowed to go anywhere or see anything. I take people as I find them, and Jack Pickford was charming. In a mature way now, I look back on this enchanting young man. He was so magnetic, and was probably the best actor in the family. I think I was much too innocent, much too young for him, but he treated me with the greatest kindness and sweetness.

"I worked for Marshall Neilan on *Bob Hampton of Placer* [1921]. I was so young. I was on ice, as he put it, and I didn't know what he meant. At first I had nothing but a sweet, young face, and Grace Kingsley, who was then very important here on the *Times,* gave me some good reviews. That had brought me to Neilan's attention.

"Marshall Neilan was a character. I don't think I want to say too much. I have the warmest feelings for him. I'll tell you, there was a while during that period of my life I was traveling in rather heady circles, but I wasn't touched because I was so young. I think, perhaps, I can tell you this. I was on the set and somebody came from another studio—I think it was Paramount—and Mr. Neilan in a loud voice called out, 'Where's Priscilla? Bring her over here.' Then he turned to the man, and said, 'We've got a virgin.' Of course, everybody laughed, and at this point I came up, and he said, 'You are a virgin, aren't you dear?' And he said, 'You go back and tell them Neilan's got a virgin.' It was a company joke. I was a joke.

"I only played a very small part in *Shadows* [1922]. I tell you I really had two careers. I went up very fast. Then certain things happened and I was very ill, and when I came back, I was very thin, and could no longer play ingenues. So I became a character ingenue. It was only a bit in *Shadows.* Marguerite de la Motte was the star, she was very, very sweet and everybody loved her. Peggy, they called her.

"I made two films over at the old Christie studios, *Hold Your Breath* and *Charley's Aunt* [1924 and 1925 respectively]. I wasn't the lead in *Charley's Aunt;* there were three girls. Sydney Chaplin was the star. He was supposed to be a bit of a chaser, but I guess I wasn't his type.

"*Drusilla with a Million* [1925] was the first picture I was featured in. It was a tearjerker, a real tearjerker. Apparently, I found it easy to play emotional roles. It's a strange thing. I was rather shy when I was young, not excessively, and I would be a little tongue-tied from time to time. But the minute I was standing on the stage and the camera was going I became the person I was playing. I remember an instance with John Barrymore.* After I was signed, he turned to me

---

*Priscilla Bonner was originally signed to portray the role of Esther Harper in *The Sea Beast*, opposite John Barrymore. This role was eventually played by Dolores Costello.

Priscilla Bonner, as Sally May Ferris, in *Drusilla with a Million* (1925).

The cast and crew of *The Red Kimono* (1925). Mrs. Wallace Reid and Priscilla Bonner are seated on the table; director Walter Lang is kneeling immediately in front of Mrs. Reid.

and said, 'Are you afraid of me?' I said, 'Yes, Mr. Barrymore.' He said, 'My friends call me Jakie,' and I said, 'Yes, Mr. Barrymore.' Then he looked at me rather quizzically, and I could see he didn't like it. So I said, 'Don't worry, it'll be all right on the set, as I'm playing the character, I'll be the character, and I won't be afraid of you then. I'm only afraid of you personally.' That didn't make much of a hit with him!

"I don't know why Mrs. Wallace Reid cast me in *The Red Kimono* [1925]. She must have interviewed many people but at that time I was what might be described as rather hot property. Walter Lang directed it. That was his first directorial assignment, and he was very anxious, but she was a great help to him. Mrs. Wallace Reid is a great lady. She's very dear to me.

"*The Red Kimono* was written by Adela Rogers St. Johns, and it was a true story. It happened in St. Louis. The heroine, whose name was Gabrielle Darley, had married, and married well, and moved away from her early life. After the film was released, she went to a picture show one day, and saw *The Red Kimono*. Even her name was used! She went to an attorney, and she sued Mrs. Wallace Reid. She got every nickel Mrs. Reid had, including the Wally Reid home in West Hol-

lywood. Of course, they didn't realize they should change the name of the girl, but it was such a dramatic story, and it was filmed exactly as it happened.

"Bessie Love did the first picture with Mrs. Wallace Reid [*Human Wreckage*], and that was about dope. Of course, you know that was what killed Wally. Everybody knows it. It's no secret—was no secret then. Mrs. Wallace Reid went through such stark tragedy with her loved one that she wanted to try and tell the world—the message could well be repeated now. She was trying to tell the world, 'Don't let it happen to another fine young man.' She was so highly regarded by the entire profession.

"She was a close friend of Adela Rogers St. Johns, and, together, they thought up what the second picture could be. It could be a crusade. Suddenly, up they came with this story that Adela Rogers St. Johns had covered, and thought it was good to go from dope to 'let those without sin cast the first stone.' Mrs. Wallace Reid appeared at the beginning and then at the end of the film. She was always on the set, always. She was a producer, and a good producer. Everyone loves her who knows her. She's a joy. She's a great lady.

"*The Red Kimono* was quite well received, and

Priscilla Bonner as Gabrielle Darley in *The Red Kimono* (1925).

so they threw together, very quickly, *The Earth Woman* [1926]. That was a cheater. I had done quite well in *The Red Kimono*, and so....

"I had a very small part in *The Strong Man* [1926]. There was a very poignant scene, just where the funny-looking man stands in front of the girl to whom he is a dream man, and she can't see him, so he always will be. She never dreamed he'd come, and she never dreamed he'd know she was blind. It's a beautiful situation, and so they didn't want a girl who was a comedienne to play it. I think that's why I was chosen. Really, it's a very small part. I only had two scenes in the whole picture.

"I'm not sure I want to talk about Harry Langdon. It was a very complicated situation. There were other people involved.

"Of course, Frank Capra was the great director, later proven, and Frank Capra directed *The Strong Man*. Harry Langdon was, in his time, compared to be as great as Chaplin, and perhaps with the right guidance, and if Capra had remained, he might have gone on, but fate intervened. Capra was gone, and there was trouble. Let it rest.

"I made two films with him, but on the second picture [*Long Pants,* 1927] there was so much trouble. Harry Langdon paid so dearly for his mistake. He was a dear man, so gentle and kind. He had very bad advice. He should have stayed with Capra, Capra would have soared with him. There were other people in there, of course. There was this woman he married, who was not a smart woman. It was a sad situation, it was a tragedy. He, like so many highly gifted men, was perhaps not too stable.

"I had a lot of bad luck on *Three Bad Men* [1926]. Olive Borden played the lead, and Olive was just beautiful, and I played the character ingenue, a very dramatic part. But I was all cut out. Olive Borden was so adorable, they used about three reels of her, and cut out everything that was dramatic in the picture. Lou Tellegen was in that picture, and he beat me with a whip. That was very dramatic, but by the time they got through, it was mostly Olive taking a bath in a barrel. They had decided to make a star of her. John Ford (the director) refused to have anything to do with the picture. It was so changed, so cut.

"*It:* Let me say I got on all right with everybody, because I'm easy-going. You see I was under contract to Mr. Langdon, and he didn't have anything

Priscilla Bonner and Alec B. Francis in *Three Bad Men* (1926).

for me to do, and so they loaned me over to Paramount. Now at that time, I had reached the point where I had been featured in several pictures, and I didn't want to support a feminine star. But I had to, and so I did it with the best grace

Clara Bow and Priscilla Bonner in *It* (1927).

73

possible. Clara Bow was very pleasant to me, and I was very pleasant to her. But you see when you support a star of the size and magnitude of Clara Bow, you play always with your left ear to the camera. That is about what it amounted to. I didn't make any trouble, I never made any trouble.

"I don't remember the dramatic scene with the baby. I always had babies, and they were taken away, or there were rain scenes, and I was dragged through the rain. You see once you come to their attention in something like that, you're stuck.

"I had a hemorrhage of the retina from a picture, a Joe Rock picture [*Outcast Souls,* 1928]. It was serious, and I didn't know it, and I kept on working. I couldn't see anything, and when I went home that night all the electric light globes in the street were pink. But I didn't complain; I was back there the next day working.

"That injury stopped me. I didn't work, and the man I was going to marry wanted me to marry. I had had a bad time on another picture, and he was pretty outraged. He said, 'Let's get married and no more work.' He was a pretty forceful man, and a very strong man. I knew I couldn't have a career and him. I had to make a decision right there. I've never worked since I was married."

9

Bebe Daniels and Ben Lyon

Bebe Daniels and Ben Lyon were the cinema screen's most popular married couple. From their marriage in 1930 until Bebe's death on March 16, 1971, they were two of the most adored stars in show business, particularly in England, where, because of their war work, they had found a special place in people's hearts. Ben subsequently married Marian Nixon, a star of silents and early talkies and the widow of William Seiter, in 1972, and they now live in the States.

Bebe began her career as a child actress her first screen appearance being in Selig's *The Common Enemy*, released on April 4, 1910. She subsequently worked for Kalem, Universal, Kay-Bee, and Vitagraph, before becoming Harold Lloyd's leading lady. She became a full-fledged star in the twenties with Paramount, appearing in, among others, *The Affairs of Anatol* (1921), *Miss Bluebeard* (1925), *Volcano* (1926), and *She's a Sheik* (1927).

Ben Lyon began his screen career in the late teens, with supporting roles in *The Slacker* (1917), *The Easiest Way* (1917), and *The Transgressor* (1918), etc. In 1919, he starred in Warner's *Open Your Eyes,* which showed "the effect of sexual disease on those who live vicious lives." It was

not surprising that after such a film he should return to the stage, coming back to the screen in the twenties. His most famous screen role was, of course, as Monte Rutledge in *Hell's Angels* (1930).

The following interview was first published in *The Silent Picture* No. 10 (Spring, 1971). It was recorded at the Lyons' London apartment.

"BD   My mother started to work as the casting director with Pathe; that's how we got into the film business. And she said, 'Whatever you do, don't mention the fact that you're in films.'

AS   Was your mother casting director at Kalem?

BD   Yes—she was casting director in several studios.

AS   I think Carlyle Blackwell was the head of the studio.

BD   That's right. I remember that I doubled for his wife, because she was afraid to ride horseback. So I doubled for her. I never had a double in my life.

AS   How did you first come to meet Hal Roach?

BD   Well, I heard he was looking for a leading lady for Harold Lloyd, and I said to my mother, 'I'm going to apply for that job.' My aunt was staying with us, my Aunt Alma, and so I asked her if I could borrow her suit as I was wearing short

Bebe Daniels.

Ben Lyon.

Bebe Daniels and Rudolph Valentino in *Monsieur Beaucaire* (1924).

Lucien Prival and Ben Lyon in *Hell's Angels* (1930).

dresses at that time. And she said, 'Of course.' So I went down, and Hal said, 'Well I like you, and if Harold likes you, fine.' So Harold came in, and he said, 'Yes—I think she's wonderful.' That's how I got the job. We used to make a picture a week, 52 pictures a year. If we wanted a holiday, we had to make two pictures a week.

AS   And as the Lloyd character developed, did you find that the character you were playing had to develop also?

BD   No. I just played the same character, but Harold changed. I worked with Hal until one day I was out to dinner with Harold Lloyd, and C. B. DeMille was in the restaurant, and he asked if he could come over as he'd like to meet me. So Harold and I went over to his table, and he said, 'How would you like to come and work with me?'

And I said, 'Well, that's very nice, but I'm very happy where I am.' And he said, 'If and when you want to come to me, just let me know.' So Hal and Harold both said, 'This is a great opportunity for you, and we think you ought to go.' Then I said, 'I'll wait till my contract expires,' which I did, and then I called up and asked if he was still interested, and he said, 'Very much so.'

So I borrowed my mother's suit, and my grandmother had brought a lot of egrets back from South America, and I had this hat with all these egrets on it, you see. So I went to his office, and he said, 'Well, I'm signing you up, but please throw that hat away.' A wonderful man—wonderful, but a funny thing about C. B. if he thought anybody was really ill, that was all right, but if he thought they were feigning being ill, he lost his temper with them. I was in *Male and Female* [1919] with Thomas Meighan. I was his favorite wife or something. I don't remember. And Gloria Swanson was the one that came along and was thrown to the lions. DeMille was a wonderful producer.

AS Of the films that you made at Paramount, which do you remember with the most affection?

BD I did a lot of films with Wallace Reid.

AS Was he showing any signs of the drug addiction that was to kill him?

BD A bit—yes. I remember they finally carried him off the set. He and Valentino were two of the nicest men I've ever known. I have never met a more modest man in my life than Rudy was. I remember we used to go horseback riding together, and I'd say, 'Come on Rudy, let's take this fence.' And he'd say, 'No, Bebe,' and I'd say, 'why?' There were quite a lot of people in the riding party, and he'd say, 'They'll think I'm showing off.' So he went back to Italy, and when he came back, I said, 'Rudy, what happened? they must have mobbed you.' He said, 'Nothing happened, because I look like every other wop on the street.' He didn't know what conceit was.

AS What sort of salary were you earning?

BD With Harold Lloyd I started at ten dollars a week, then went to 25, then went to 50. I don't think I ever made more than $100 a week with Harold Lloyd. Then I went to Paramount, and I think I started there at $1,000 a week. Then I went over to RKO, and they said they couldn't afford to pay my salary, would I take a percentage, and so I said yes. I had a percentage on *Rio Rita* [1929]. I had ten percent of everything it made—made a bomb on it.

AS Who were your close friends in Hollywood?

Georges Renevant, Bebe Daniels, and John Boles in *Rio Rita* (1929).

BD Motion picture people—Thomas Meighan and his wife. In those days—in talking pictures—you couldn't go out at night really, because you had to get up so early, and you had all your dialogue to learn. In silent pictures, we were able to go out at night. They were very nice days.

AS I believe you were a close friend of Marion Davies?

BD A lovely, wonderful girl. I was very fond of Marion; very hospitable, very generous type. A lovely girl. We used to go horseback riding together. We used to have picnics on the beach.

AS Do you think that Hearst had a bad influence on her career in that he prevented her from playing the roles that best suited her?

BD No, I don't think so.

BL I think, probably, she did the roles that she wanted to do. He only financed the company, Cosmopolitan. He was directly responsible for making her a star.

BD I think she was very satisfied in what she was doing. She never said anything to either of us, and we were very close, I think that if she had felt that way she would have said something about it.

AS When you were at Paramount, were you allowed to choose your own films?

BD To a certain extent—yes. Only, of course, when I worked with DeMille, I didn't choose those. He was the big white chief.

AS When did you first take up scriptwriting?

BD From early days—I mean when I worked with Harold, we never had a script. We always went on location and thought up things, and that really started it. Then, when I was working at Realart, it was very difficult to get the right kind of writers, so I would write most of the stuff myself. I didn't take credit for it. Then, when I went back and produced for Hal Roach, I wrote both those films, and then the studio went out of business. *The Fabulous Joe* [1947], that was the story of a talking dog. And you know we had auditions for dogs, and there was one dog that came in—he wasn't the type—but he could really talk. He could say several things, but, as I say, he wasn't the type, so we got another dog. At Realart, I used to work in the cutting room as well.

AS Was this encouraged by the studio?

BD Well, they didn't seem to mind. I used to go in and splice films, and work on them. Somebody had to cut it, and I would say, 'You've cut it in the wrong place.' They would say, 'Well, you better go and cut it yourself.' So I would. We worked sort of as a unit, nothing like it today.

AS You went to jail for seven days, I believe, in the Twenties?

BD Ten days. I got off one day for good behaviour. You see, I used to speed all the time, and my uncle would say—he was a newspaper man and very close to the courts—'How many tickets did you get today, Bebe?' And I'd say, 'Four,' and he would say, 'Only four? You're slipping.' So I was pretty spoilt. I was riding in a car with Jack Dempsey and my mother, and this speed cop came along, and he said, 'You know we put people in jail for going that fast.' And I said, 'Oh, don't be silly, my uncle won't let me go to jail.' So I phoned up Uncle Jack, and he said, 'Where are you, Bebe?' I said, 'Santa Ana.' He said, 'Bebe, you are in the wrong county.'

So, I had to go to jail. Had a trial by jury, and had to go to jail for nine days, one day off for good behaviour. My cell was furnished by the best decorator in town, my meals were served by a waiter in full dress, and every time anyone called to see me, the jailer would come in and say, 'Miss Daniels, so-and-so to see you.' And I'd say, 'Tell them I'm not in.' He said, 'Look Miss Daniels I've done everything in the world for you, but I can't say that.' It turned out very well, because it could have been very serious. Then, afterwards I made a film called *The Speed Girl* [1921], which really capitalized on it.

AS How did you come to make *Rio Rita* [1929]?

BD I was with Paramount, and Paramount was letting all of its artists go because talking pictures were coming in. They didn't even take tests of anyone's voice to see if they could talk. They just wanted stage people, and stage people didn't appeal to the public because they didn't know them. So RKO called up, and said would I go over there, so I went over, and I said to Bill LeBaron, 'I hear you're making *Rio Rita*.' And he said, 'This is a singing picture, Bebe,' and I said, 'Well, I can sing, Bill. Would you like me to take a test?' He said, 'Of course not, if you can sing, you can do the part.' So he didn't even take a test of me. We shot it in 24 shooting days.

AS I haven't seen *Rio Rita*, but I have seen *Dixiana* [1930], which I must confess seems rather dated.

BD Oh that was terrible. It was dated then, believe me. The leading man was awful.

Bebe Daniels in *Dixiana* (1930).

BL   You see after Bebe made *Rio Rita,* which was really the forerunner of the lavish musicals, Bebe wanted to continue making films with John Boles. If you get a successful team, keep them together, but somehow or other LeBaron or RKO had some trouble with Boles.

BD   No, they didn't.

BL   I don't know why they didn't use him then.

BD   I know why. Because the wife went to see this other man in opera, and she thought he was wonderful. And I said, 'Bill, you're making a grave mistake. I know this man is going to photograph like a lizard; he has no appeal at all; no personality.' 'Bebe,' he said, 'I have faith in you and I have faith in me.' What are you going to say to that? And it's true. He had faith in me, so I had to do it, whether I wanted to do it or not.

AS   How did you two come to meet?

BL   We met around 1925, I think it was, at a big dinner party in New York, and I'd only been in pictures about a year-and-a-half, and I was very enthused. I was very lucky; I stepped from the New York stage into leading roles in films. Everything was going so marvellously for me so that evening I met Bebe I was so enthused over the film work, I spent my evening telling her about the films I had done and my work. She thought I was the most egotistical man she'd ever met.

BD   Couldn't stand him.

BL   It wasn't ego or anything—it was just enthusiasm. So, therefore, I didn't see her again until about 1928 in California when we met at another dinner party, and then about late 1928 we became engaged, and got married in 1930.

AS   On *Counsellor at Law* [1933], what type of director was William Wyler to work for?

BD   Very good, but he used to shoot everything in one take, and John Barrymore would have speeches that long! I mean no one could memorize speeches like that. But Wyler insisted, and if Barrymore would fluff, he'd take it again. And I remember Ben came on the set one day, and what was it—take what?

BL   I waited for the red light to go off, and finally it went off, and I opened the door to go in, and they said, 'Quiet everybody, action, production so-and-so, take 47.' I heard 'Take 47' and froze. My God, if I made a sound, and I spoilt it, it will be take 48, and they'll kill me. It wasn't just so much a question of long speeches, Bebe, Willy Wyler would shoot, four, five, six minute scenes with Barrymore, and it was too much for him at that time.

AS   You starred opposite Douglas Fairbanks in *Reaching for the Moon* [1931]. Seeing his films today, one can't help feeling that he must have been a very conceited person.

BD   Oh that's not true at all! Not at all. He was very easy to work with. Of course, he was a good fencer, and we were both very interested in fencing, and I had a very wonderful collection of swords, and so did he. We had a lot in common.

AS   How did you come to settle in this country?

BD   Originally we came over here on account of a kidnap scare in America. This nurse was going to kidnap Barbara.

BL   It's a very complicated story to tell. The fact was she was unhappily married, and apparently she must have been slightly mental to think up such a plan. She figured by kidnapping Barbara, that when the story broke in the papers, then she would have been a heroine by finding Barbara and bringing Barbara back. This sounds very complicated, I know, but basically this is the idea, and sympathy would have been built up, and it might have brought her together again with her husband. She went to Pinkertons, a private agency, and told them in advance of her plan—to establish the fact that maybe she wasn't going to do any harm to the child. Anyway, the district attorney advised us to get out of the country until it blew over. Bebe was under contract to Warners, I was under contract to M-G-M. We were both between pictures, so we came over here, and made a personal appearance at the Palladium for three weeks. Somebody said would you go to Glasgow, Manchester—we were hams. We loved it, walking out on stage, getting laughs and applause, which you didn't get in the studio. We were thrilled by it.

AS   Was this the first time you'd played together on the stage?

BL   Oh no, we'd done a play in America called *Hollywood Holiday*. We did that in 1934 in Chicago and Boston and Philadelphia. It was a comedy, Bebe, myself and a friend of mine named Skeets Gallagher, who was quite a well-known comedian. We produced it with the idea of taking it to New York, but we never thought it was strong enough for New York.

BD   I think we were going to New York; we were booked for New York, but I got measles. My mother was always proud of the fact that I didn't get any children's diseases, so I got them all after I was grown-up.

BL   Yes, mother used to say, 'My baby never had mumps, never had measles, chicken pox, any of those things.' After we got married she had everything!

AS   Can you tell me something of your wartime career together?

BD   We went to Normandy. I think I was the first woman in Normandy.

BL   Yes, Bebe was decorated by the American government for her services with the Legion of Merit, which is the highest decoration that America can give a civilian, only awarded for services rendered under fire. Her official citation specifies that she was the first woman civilian to land in Normandy—that was D-Day plus 15. She went over and recorded the American wounded,

Douglas Fairbanks, Sr., and Bebe Daniels in *Reaching for the Moon* (1931).

showing the speed and efficiency of the chain of evacuation. How a man could be wounded in Normandy in the morning, and be in a general hospital in England in the afternoon. It gave great comfort to mothers and fathers and sweethearts back in America, who imagined their loved ones being wounded on the battlefield and left to die.

Later in Italy, she recorded the British wounded, as well as the Americans down there. Prior to that, we, of course, like all the other artists were doing variety here, war broke out, and we started entertaining the troops and factories, and we thought this was rather silly. Drive through the night, out to some outpost, and you got about 35 men to entertain. So we thought let's do something that will cover millions of people, and Bebe wrote a sample script called *Hi Gang,* which we submitted to the B.B.C. They liked it, put it on the air for six weeks, said if it catches on, we'll keep it on.

And it ran for 1940, 1941 and 1942, until I went into service with the US airforce as a pilot. (I'd been in the airforce reserve since 1931). An American officer cannot entertain, that's one of the rules of the American army. So we had to give up the *Hi Gang* show, but Bebe went on entertaining. She organized the American Oversea Artists, which was the first group to entertain the American soldiers over here. And that's about it!

BD   I did *Panama Hattie* too.

BL   Oh yes, and we did *Gangway* at the Palladium, which ran for 47 weeks, and *Haw Haw* at the Holborn which ran 37 weeks.

AS   How did *Life with the Lyons* come about?

BD   Well, at the time, they didn't have any family shows in this country, and we had our children, and so we approached the B.B.C. about it, and so we did *Life with the Lyons*.

BL   It was the first show with a genuine family

Ben, Bebe, and Richard in *Life with the Lyons.*

—ran from November, 1950 to 1961.

BD   We used to get letters from families saying will you please tell Richard not to run up and down the stairs, because my kid did that the other day and broke his leg.

AS   It didn't make a good transition to television did it?

BL   Well I'll tell you, it's like reading a book. You read the book, and then see the film, and in all probability you're disappointed. To me it's a pity—I know this sounds silly and no one will agree with me—that television ever came in, because at least with radio you sit down and listen and you mentally produce the show to your own one hundred percent satisfaction. Well, having heard *Life with the Lyons* on radio for so many years, and then suddenly seeing it, people had a different idea of the home, of the surroundings, of the whole situation, and it's very hard to live up to it. Although we did 32 TV shows for B.B.C. and Associated Redifusion."

10
Jetta Goudal

Jetta Goudal was one of those exotic, beautiful creatures, who graced the cinema screens during the twenties. She was never quite as popular as Pola Negri or Barbara La Marr, but many would say she was a better actress, and she was certainly far above the publicity outrages of Miss Negri.

Herbert Howe called her "a Parisian Chinese Lily," and in *Photoplay* (August 1923) wrote: "She is a perfect visualization of Hergesheimer's *Pilar*—that water lily bloom, so densely pale, whose lips of artificial carmine were like the applied petals of a geranium. With the candor and charm of the French she has a strange beauty of Oriental cast. She might be slavic. There is a marked resemblance to Nazimova in her smile and the inflection of her voice. She speaks with delicate gestures of her hands. Her fingers are long and slim with polished, painted nails."

The mention of Hergesheimer's *La Pilar* is no idle reference, for it was as this character in John S. Robertson's production of *The Bright Shawl* that Jetta Goudal made her first screen appearance. Writing of the screen version of the Joseph Hergesheimer novel, released on April 9, 1923, *Moving Picture World* (April 28, 1923) commented, "A unique and excellent portrayal is that of a newcomer, Jetta Goudal, in the role of the almond-eyed vamp, born in China, who is a spy for the Spaniards." Praise of her first screen appearance came from all sides. Alan Dale (critic of the *New York American*) wrote that "Miss Goudal was a treat to behold as well as a clever little actress," while Harriette Underhill (of the *New York Tribune*) described her as "perfectly fascinating....Never have we seen so sweetly sinister a figure as this strange Chinese person."

Jetta Goudal was born in Versailles, France, on July 12, 1901. The daughter of a Parisian lawyer, she was more than adequately educated, attending schools in France and Liege, Belgium. At the age of fifteen, convinced that her parents would never allow her the stage career for which she longed, Jetta ran away from home and joined a touring stock company.

At the age of eighteen, she came to the States and embarked on a theatrical career here. She appeared in *The Hero, The Elton Case,* and *Simon Called Peter,* and became, for one so young, a highly successful stage actress. The distinguished critic Arthur Hornblow, writing of *The Hero* in the May 1921 issue of *Theatre Magazine*, noted that "Grant Mitchell, as the real hero of the play

Jetta Goudal.

—heroic in an honest, loving, plodding way —tinges his role with pathos, as does Jetta Goudal, the betrayed little foreigner.''

Director John S. Robertson saw her on the stage, and asked her to make a test for *The Bright Shawl*. Miss Goudal was not overly enamoured of the screen, but she accepted the role, partly because it required a trip to Cuba, away from the cold of New York, which she hated. (Ill-health was constantly to dog Miss Goudal during the twenties, but however sick she might be in reality, in film after film she always turned in a fine performance.)

The Bright Shawl was not released until April 1923, but in the meantime, Goudal, at the request of director Sidney Olcott, played the role of a tubercular woman of the slums in *Timothy's Quest*, released in the autumn of 1922. In this charming tale of a young boy and girl's search for parental love, Miss Goudal may be glimpsed in the opening scenes of the film.

Timothy's Quest was followed by *The Green Goddess*, directed again by Sidney Olcott, and released in the summer of 1923. In this first film version of the celebrated melodrama—it was remade in 1930—Jetta essayed the small role of the

Jetta Goudal in her first major screen role, as La Pilar, in *The Bright Shawl* (1923).

Jetta Goudal and ''Baby'' Helen Rowland in *Timothy's Quest* (1922).

Ayah. Despite the film's boasting a leading man of the magnitude of George Arliss, Miss Goudal received considerable critical attention. Harriette Underhill, writing in the *New York Tribune,* noted, "Next to Mr. Arliss we liked that intriguing little French actress Jetta Goudal...With the exception of Pola Negri, we never have seen anyone of the screen possessed of such charm, grace and magnetism. If we were a manager we should seek her out, beg her to sign a contract and put her name up in electric lights. 'Eventually—Why not now?' The only trouble with Miss Goudal's performance is that there is not half enough of it." In the *Morning Telegraph,* Louella Parsons wrote, "Jetta Goudal, who will probably be heard from, contributes one of the best performances on the screen. As for looks, well, we will say that it is not the place to take a husband and sweetheart who fall for feminine beauty. She is some looker. We are willing to bet our money on her."

As it happened, Miss Goudal was sought out by Paramount, and, in 1924, signed a three-picture contract with them. The contract was largely a result of director Paul Bern having seen her in *The Elton Case* on stage, and deciding she was exactly whom he needed to play the lead in his new production, *Open All Night.* Indeed Bern told Goudal, "I will not do it without you." Not only was *Open All Night* Jetta's first Paramount picture, it was also her first film in California.

Yet again, reviews were excellent. The former screen actress Florence Lawrence, then drama critic on the *Los Angeles Examiner*, wrote, "Goudal will stand out in the minds of everyone who sees the play by reason of her dramatic entrances and the praise and intrigue of her acting. Costumes and gestures alike display a finesse which marks her for a brilliant screen career." Willis Goldbeck, who was responsible for the screenplay, cabled Jetta after the production's New York opening, "I have nothing but warmest praise for your splendid performance in *Open All Night*. First running of picture has raised our hopes." Some fifty years later, Goldbeck again saw the film, and at the picture's close turned to Goudal and commented, "You sure gave a performance."

During 1924, Jetta starred in her two other Paramount features, *The Spaniard* and *Salome of the Tenements,* both released early in 1925. In the former, directed by Raoul Walsh, Miss Goudal

showed her versatility by portraying an English girl. In Sidney Olcott's *Salome of the Tenements,* she displayed even greater versatility, playing Sonya Mendel in her rise from a ten-year-old child of New York's East Side tenements to that city's high society. Miss Goudal comments, "I always considered my performance as the ten-year-old child as my 'tour de force.'" Children from the New York slums were used as extras in the film, and Jetta recalls, "Even the street children, all brought in from the ghetto, did not realize that I was not one of them, which was and which I considered one of the greatest compliments."

Of her performance, Florence Lawrence, in the March 9, 1925, issue of the *Los Angeles Examiner,* wrote, "The role is a big one for Jetta Goudal, and she shows from the first reel that she's amply fitted for it. Emotionally and dramatically this young woman swept her spectators with her work. She was most amazing perhaps in the role of the twelve-year-old girl, and her daring impudence, her fighting and squabbling as the little East Side orphan was a far cry, indeed, from the ultra sophisticated, beautifully gowned and exotically environed roles in which she has been seen heretofore.

Throughout the picture Miss Goudal registered with vivid art. Her personality was always outstanding, and her attainment of her objective in the story episode quick and comprehensible to every spectator."

In 1925 Miss Goudal's Paramount contract was at an end, and she signed a long-term contract with Cecil B. DeMille, requiring a maximum of three pictures a year. The producer had recently contracted to release his films through Producers' Distributing Corporation, committing himself to producing, but not directing, a certain number of films a year. Jetta was featured in DeMille's second P.D.C. release, *The Coming of Amos,* directed by Paul Sloane, which she recalls "was a heavy picture, but it was a perfectly charming picture."

Jetta Goudal's first—and only—starring role under DeMille's direction came with *The Road to Yesterday*, released on November 15, 1925. Jetta played Malena Paulton, opposite Joseph Schildkraut as Kenneth Paulton, in this tale of two couples hurled back in time as a result of a train crash. The crash was possibly the best thing in the feature; *Variety* (December 2, 1925) called it "the

Rod La Rocque and Jetta Goudal in *The Coming of Amos* (1925).

A posed shot of Joseph Schildkraut and Jetta Goudal in *The Road to Yesterday* (1925).

Jetta Goudal as the afflicted woman in *The King of Kings,* one of the scenes cut from the 1927 production.

me on Via Doloroso in *The King of Kings,* but I have been forced to eliminate even many major scenes...."

Three Jetta Goudal features were released during 1926. *Three Faces East,* directed by Rupert Julian, and *Her Man O'War,* directed by Frank Urson, were also De Mille productions. The latter was claimed by the De Mille studios to have been Miss Goudal's first starring vehicle, which provided her "with a splendid tragi-comic role, in which she proves her remarkable versatility and the unlimited range of her emotional powers." *Paris at Midnight,* released on April 18, 1926, was directed by E. Mason Hopper, and was a Frances Marion production; Miss Marion also wrote the script.

Miss Goudal was responsible for the writing of a new ending for *Three Faces East,* as she was for a new ending of a later film, *The Forbidden Woman.* Working with Frances Marion, on *Paris at Midnight,* was a particularly pleasant experience for Jetta: "There was nothing in *Paris at Midnight* that I wanted changed because Frances Marion was an intelligent woman. She and I got along famously, appreciating each other to the fullest."

In 1927, Jetta Goudal appeared in three final films under her DeMille contract: *White Gold, Fighting Love,* and *The Forbidden Woman.* The first was possibly her most important film, directed by William K. Howard. He did not originally want Miss Goudal in the leading role of Dol-

greatest train wreck scene ever shot." (Incidentally, Miss Goudal had no double during the shooting of this sequence.)

After completion of *The Road to Yesterday,* DeMille offered Jetta the starring role in *The Volga Boatman,* but, after hearing the storyline, she turned it down. Jetta did, however, work on the producer's most famous film of the twenties, *The King of Kings.* She was originally to have portrayed Mary Magdalene, but that role went to Jacqueline Logan. De Mille then cast her as an afflicted woman, but her footage was subsequently cut from the film. In a letter dated February 28, 1927, De Mille wrote her, "It is with much regret that I am writing to tell you that it has been necessary, on account of footage, to eliminate the very lovely piece of work that you did for

Jetta Goudal as Cherie Schultz in *Her Man O' War* (1926).

ores Carson: "Life was not easy while we were doing it," she recalls. However, Goudal and Howard came in for some quite extraordinary praise. Typical is the following from the *Los Angeles Times* of February 20, 1927: "Heretofore, there have been many who felt that Miss Goudal, while undoubtedly talented, was lacking in many of the qualities that make for wide appeal with American audiences. In none of her earlier pictures has she been revealed as a woman of real flesh and blood. Not that she was ethereal, or anything like that, but she apparently could not achieve the feat of convincing that she was a warm and vibrant personality.

"Howard has humanized her. He has brought something to the surface that makes her a woman of charm and beauty. One feels her as a presence to whom the sympathies could be extended without any great expenditure of effort.

"Her portrayal of the woman in the heat and sand and loneliness of an Arizona sheep ranch has a sharply etched quality that is memorable. Her struggle against the drabness of her new existence, and the relentless hatred of her husband's father; her fine courage in the face of a cooling ardor and a soul-crushing indifference, are phases of character—vividly impressive."

Frances Marion also saw *White Gold,* and wrote Jetta: "Mr. [Victor] Seastrom and I ran *White Gold.* It is an excellent picture, and what beautiful work you did in it. We were so enthusiastic—both wanted you to know of our appreciation and enthusiasm. You are a great actress and a sweet, charming woman."

Some twenty-five years or so after the film's release, William K. Howard acquired the remake rights. He telephoned Jetta, and told her that he couldn't shoot the picture again without her. She refused, and *White Gold* was never remade.

Jetta Goudal's contract with DeMille was terminated with a very famous law suit, involving, among other things, DeMille's assertions that Miss Goudal was a very temperamental and difficult actress to work with. The courts found very much in Jetta's favor. She had brought suit claiming that she had been dismissed by DeMille in September 1927, despite her contract's promising her employment until 1930. The courts awarded her $31,000 in damages.

At this point, it is perhaps worthwhile pointing out that the story of Jetta Goudal's temperamen-

tality was originally thought up by Paramount's publicity department. It was not too long before that studio, and others, began believing their own publicity. "They have accused me of many things, but never of being dumb," comments Jetta.

While her lawsuit was in progress, Jetta was also very active in Equity's fight for the unionization of film players. "Joan of Ark of Equity," she was dubbed by her fellow actors.

1928 saw Jetta working at M-G-M on the Marion Davies vehicle, *The Cardboard Lover,* directed by Robert Z. Leonard. The highlight of the production was a biting parody of Miss Goudal by Miss Davies. (Interestingly, a year later, Lupe Velez was to be seen impersonating Jetta on a personal appearance tour with *Lady of the Pavements.*) *The New York Times* (September 3, 1928) commented: "Miss Davies' impersonation of Miss Goudal is so remarkable that one can hardly be quite certain that she is not Miss Goudal." Jetta certainly did not find such impersonations offensive, indeed she herself designed the costume for Marion Davies to wear in her parody.

A surprise visitor to the set of *The Cardboard Lover* was Greta Garbo, who came not to be entertained by Marion Davies, but to watch Jetta Goudal act. Some two years earlier, Nazimova had visited the set of *The Road to Yesterday* for the same reason.

D. W. Griffith directed Jetta in *Lady of the Pavements,* released by United Artists on February 16, 1929. The film has Miss Goudal as a French Countess take a woman of the streets (Lupe Velez) and train her to win the love of the man (William Boyd) who had turned down Goudal's advances after finding her in the arms of her Emperor. It was a role to which Jetta brought a hauteur and a grandeur that was uniquely her own. Miss Goudal recalls that she, on request from Griffith, designed all her own costumes, and that the director insisted that they "should be the most beautiful ever seen."

Jetta became increasingly interested in her hobby of interior decoration, and more and more disenchanted with her film career. In 1929, she appeared in only one other film, *Le Spectre Vert,* a French-language version of M-G-M's *The Unholy Night,* directed by Jacques Feyder. (The American film was directed by Lionel Barrymore, and Jetta's role of Lady Effra was portrayed by Dorothy Sebastian.)

Her first professional assignment as an interior decorator was on Paul Bern's home, and it was here that she met Harold Grieve.* The couple were married in October 1930. Miss Goudal returned to the screen only once, in 1932, to play opposite Will Rogers in David Butler's production of *Business and Pleasure*. This return to the screen was only to please her husband.

Jetta Goudal Grieve still lives in Hollywood with her husband. They are both retired. Looking back on her career, she commented, "I have pleasant memories, and I also have many unpleasant memories....I've always tried in life to play the game fair and square. At least I can ask for 'A' for effort.

Harold Grieve was responsible for the interior design of the Hollywood U.S.O.

*Harold Grieve was one of the silent screen's finest art directors. A Hollywood boy, he began his career in Metro's draughting room. It was director Rex Ingram who recognized his talents, and allowed him to display such talents on *The Prisoner of Zenda* (1922). Grieve also worked on many other films, including *Scaramouche* (1923), *Dorothy Vernon of Haddon Hall* (1924), *Lady Windermere's Fan* (1925), and *So This Is Paris* (1926). He was responsible for the props and costumes for the oriental sequences in Douglas Fairbank's *The Thief of Bagdad* (1924), and also designed the costumes for *Ben-Hur* (1925).

He left the film industry in 1926, and became an interior decorator, responsible for the interior design of the homes of many Hollywood personalities including Bing Crosby, Blanche Sweet, John Gilbert, Colleen Moore, Ernst Lubitsch, Cecil B. DeMille, Hal Roach, Edith Head, and Walt Disney. In 1931, he was called upon to decorate Miriam Hopkins's studio dressing room. Harold Grieve's most famous work is probably Colleen Moore's Doll's House, which he worked on between 1929 and 1930. His most recent work was the interior design for the 1973 Bob Hope Hollywood USO.

Harold Grieve's set for Rex Ingram's 1923 production of *Scaramouche*. Principals Lewis Stone and Alice Terry may be seen.

A sketch by Harold Grieve of one of his sets for Ernst Lubitsch's 1926 production of *So This Is Paris*.

11
Ralph Graves

Actor, director, screenwriter and producer, Ralph Graves wore all four caps during his long and active career in the film industry.

Born in Cleveland, Ohio, on January 23, 1900, Graves looks back on his childhood with mixed emotions: "I was kind of a discarded person. I was born of a good father and a questionable mother. I hope my father was what I think he was. He had a lot of money, and left some kind of inheritance. There was a divorce, and my mother married again. I was excommunicated from high school, and I wanted to get away from this family, so I got on a freight-train or something, and high-tailed it to Chicago."

In Chicago, Ralph entered a contest run by Universal to find a new leading man for Violet Mersereau. "I was a fat-faced, good-looking kid," says Graves. He and another man won the contest, and the offer of a Universal contract, but not, as advertised, a role opposite Miss Mersereau. Louella Parsons, then a Chicago newspaperwoman, stepped in, and found Graves a job with the Essanay Company, whose studio was located in Chicago.

His first major role was as "the callow youth" opposite Mary MacLane in *Men Who Have Made*

An early portrait of Ralph Graves.

94

Love to Me, released early in 1918. Miss MacLane had gained a certain amount of notoriety with her autobiography, and Essanay had decided to film it. *Variety* (February 1, 1918) commented that "Miss MacLane's supporting cast does well with what has been given it to do," but of the star herself, *Variety* continued, "It is apparent that Miss MacLane wasn't gobbled up by Essanay because of her film-acting abilities."

Before the release of *Men Who Have Made Love to Me*, Ralph Graves had left Essanay and Chicago for New York, where he played at the Fort Lee Studios of the World Company in *Tinsel*, opposite Kitty Gordon. He also worked for Maurice Tourneur in *Sporting Life*. The latter was

Graves's first important screen role, and as a result of it, Tourneur also featured him in *The White Heather*, released in 1919. Ralph recalls that as a result of his role as an amateur boxer in *Sporting Life*, "Douglas Fairbanks invited me out to meet him. I was a nobody, and suddenly being around Douglas Fairbanks gave you an aura, a distinction you didn't really deserve."

Universal brought Graves out to Hollywood, and featured him opposite Ella Hall. From Universal, Ralph went under contract to D. W Griffith.

"Mr. Griffith, who was not in any way a lover of men, seemed to take some kind of interest in me. I was no actor; I'd had no kind of training. Appar-

Ralph Graves and Carol Dempster in *Dream Street* (1921).

ently, I was a good-looking man to Griffith. I was a new kind of character. I'm not putting him down, but I was a little above the movies. I used to buy my clothes at Brooks Brothers. I looked different to Griffith. He used to wear horrible clothes and murder the King's English, which I didn't, and he took an interest in me, and immediately signed me up to a contract.''

Ralph Graves was featured in three Griffith-directed films: *Scarlet Days* (as Randolph), *The Greatest Question* (as John Hilton), and *Dream Street* (as Spike McFadden). The last, released in 1921, was his only starring role, opposite Carol Dempster. After *Dream Street* was shot, a song, also titled ''Dream Street,'' was added, using Kellum's Talking Picture process, a sound-on-disc system. Graves remembers, ''It was recorded in New York. I recorded the song, and they cut the film into it. As I remember, this was an event. We knew that. There was no belief then in the work. Nobody knew if it would work or not. I sang it, and I was amazed at my beautiful voice. I have a gorgeous voice, but nobody else knows it.''

After *Dream Street,* Graves was avalanched with offers. He had been making $450 dollars a week with Griffith, and suddenly, outsiders were offering him five thousand dollars a week. Graves went to consult with the director. ''He kissed me, and said, 'Go on, take it.' I wish I hadn't now.''

''He was mad at me for telling Carol Dempster not to get mixed up with old men. She'd destroy herself. I used to give imitations of her, and he caught me at it once. You know, I used to have an apartment on Fifth Avenue, and I used to walk over to his hotel, and ride with him up to Mamaroneck [the Griffith studio in Connecticut] in his car. All the way from the Claridge Hotel in New York. He was the greatest!

''He used to come to our house later. We had lost a half-a-million dollars by then, but we were still living in some half-baked affluence in Balboa. Here is the greatest man in the film business, and he took a bus! What a horrible thing! Monstrous system we have where people with inventive genius are relegated to living in a dump, like some cheap, crummy, unbelievable, sordid hotel, eating garbage for breakfast. This great man relegated to that. Nobody in the film industry ever did anything for him. What did I ever do for him—or what would anyone do for me? I could be walking down Hollywood Boulevard right now. Nobody gives a Goddam.''

Mabel Normand and Ralph Graves in *The Extra Girl* (1923).

In 1922, Ralph Graves settled down to a career as a popular, and reliable, leading man, playing opposite, among others, Colleen Moore (*Come On Over*), Miriam Cooper (*Kindred of the Dust*), Marjorie Daw (*The Long Chance*), Marguerite De La Motte (*The Jilt*), Bessie Love (*The Ghost Patrol*), and Gloria Swanson (*Prodigal Daughters*).

From 1923 through 1926, he was under contract to Mack Sennett. Graves played opposite Mabel Normand in the feature-length *The Extra Girl,* directed by F. Richard Jones, whose career is long overdue for study. Graves was also featured in a series of two-reel comedies, including *Don't Tell Dad* (released August 2, 1925), *Good Morning Madam* (released October 18, 1925), *The Window Dummy* (released December 13, 1925), *Meet My Girl* (released March 7, 1926), and *A Yankee Doodle Duke* (released May 30, 1926).

''Oh yes, I had an unholy relationship with Mack Sennett. I was so close to Mack Sennett....The world always thought that young actors were always out looking for dames. We were looking for them, but not the kind of dames you could get. Two years of my life—every day, every night—were spent with Mack Sennett.''

In 1927 Ralph Graves turned to directing, under Harry Cohn's supervision at Columbia. He now claims that he decided to go behind the camera because he was losing both his hair and his sex appeal, reasons that are hardly realistic in view of his continued work as an actor after his directorial debut. During 1927 he directed *Rich Men's Sons* (with Graves and Shirley Mason), *The Kid Sister*

Ralph Graves as a Mack Sennett leading man.

(with Marguerite De La Motte), and *The Swell-Head* (with Graves and Mildred Harris). At Warner Brothers, in the same year, be both wrote and directed *A Reno Divorce,* featuring himself and May McAvoy. *A Reno Divorce* was not Graves's first attempt at writing; as early as 1917 he had written a scenario for the Essanay Company.

Graves developed a close relationship with Frank Capra at Columbia. He was featured in four Capra productions: *That Certain Thing* (1928), *Submarine* (1928), *Flight* (1929), and *Ladies of Leisure* (1930). He also wrote the original story for *Flight*. "He was one of my gag-writers at Mack Sennett, recalls Graves. ''He was a very delightful guy. A wonderful director. I brought him over from Mack Sennett to Harry Cohn.''

In the early thirties, Graves drifted away from acting and became a production executive at M-G-M, working closely with Irving Thalberg. He now lives in retirement in Santa Barbara.

Ralph Graves is a very outspoken man. He is a refreshing change from many silent stars, who are out-of-touch so completely with the present. I feel the following story concerning Rudolph Valentino, better than any other, gives an insight into Ralph Graves:

"I knew Rudolfo. He worked around the Griffith studios, and couldn't get a job because he was a Goddam foreigner. He used to come to the Alexandria Hotel and sit with us. He was a wonderful dancer, and women always wanted to dance with him, but they always used to complain that that guy never pays the check. Nobody had any sympathy for him. Nobody had any use for him until Bingo, *The Four Horsemen of the Apocalypse*. He had the most unhappy life because he married these women who were not adaptable. So sad and unbelievable, and the most delightful and wonderful person that ever lived. He was always looked down on. We always look down on Black people and uneducated people. Make yourself try and discount the Nixons and the John Waynes. Just thinking about them makes me want to throw up.''

12
Alice Terry

No one had a less pretentious approach to being a film star than Alice Terry. She entered films because it seemed an easy way to earn a living. Becoming a star and marrying her director, she took in her stride. When she became bored with making movies, she quit without a backward glance.

Above all, Alice Terry enjoyed having fun and making the best of life, and the easiest way to accomplish these aims was to star in films. The chore of making films was to be gotten over as quickly as possible in order to enjoy the excitement of living. At the height of her fame, a year or two after her marriage to director Rex Ingram, Alice recalled for me that she was always anxious to find an excuse to take a break from filming. Ingram's chief aversion was to Louis B. Mayer. He would never allow Mayer's name on his productions, they were always Metro-Goldwyn releases. Alice would always scan the publicity material on each of Rex's films in the hope that she would come across Mayer's name. Such a mention brought to Ingram's attention would always result in cancellation of shooting for at least a week, while Ingram alternated between ranting and sulking. She told *Photoplay* (September

Two of Hollywood's most beautiful people: director Rex Ingram and his bride, actress Alice Terry.

1923), "I am content, when leaving the studios, to lock Alice Terry in the dressing room and become Mrs. Rex Ingram."

Alice Terry was born Alice Taaffe in Vincennes, Indiana in 1901, and was educated there and in Los Angeles, to which she came in 1915. She had no theatrical training. (Confusion with a Vitagraph actress, also named Alice Terry, has resulted in many biographical entries listing her birthplace as Washington, D.C., and her being credited with a stage career in that city.)

A girlfriend suggested Alice should try and get extra work at the studios, which she did with the Thomas Ince Company. Occasionally, Alice would achieve small parts, as in the 1916 Ince production of *Not My Sister*. Of her performance, *Photoplay* (September 1916) wrote, "She is an added starter and looks very promising."

However, film work was never anything very important in Alice's young life. Her friend Claire Du Brey obtained positions for both of them in the Universal stock company at twenty five dollars a week, but Alice preferred to stay with Ince at eighteen dollars a week, simply because she had a crush on a boy at Ince, and didn't want to be away from him all day. So disillusioned with acting did Alice become at one time, that she went into the cutting rooms at Lasky, but recalled, "The daily grind proved even more disheartening."

It was her future husband, Rex Ingram, who was responsible for Alice Taaffe's rise to stardom, when he cast her in his 1920 Metro production of *Hearts Are Trumps,* and renamed her Alice Terry. "The part of Dora Woodberry fits Miss Terry like a beautifully tailored suit," he told *Moving Picture World* (June 12, 1920). *Hearts Are Trumps* probably marked the first time that the dark-haired Miss Terry wore a blonde wig, a wig she was to favor for all her future films.

Production began on Rex Ingram's most famous and important film, *The Four Horsemen of the Apocalypse,* in December 1919. Alice Terry, according to *Moving Picture World* (August 7, 1920, was the first of the all-star cast to be chosen. Just as the production made leading man Rudolph Valentino (in the role of Julio Desnoyers) a star, it also rocketed to stardom Alice Terry (in the role of Marguerite Laurier).

Based on the novel by Vicente Blasco-Ibanez, the film was an instantaneous success. Robert E. Sherwood in *Life* magazine (March 24, 1921) wrote, "*The Four Horsemen of the Apocalypse* will be hailed as a great dramatic achievement; one which deserves—more than any other picture play that the war inspired—to be handed down to generations yet unborn....*The Four Horsemen of the Apocalypse* is a living, breathing answer to those who still refuse to take motion pictures seriously.

Its production lifts the silent drama to an artistic plane that it has never touched before."

In *Moving Picture World* (February 21, 1912), Edward Weitzel wrote, "It has that perfect blend of laughter and tears which is the goal of the dramatist, and it marks the advent of a major craftsman." Said the *Los Angeles Times*, "Alice Terry is emotionally triumphant in her role."

Rex Ingram and Alice Terry followed *The Four Horsemen of the Apocalypse* with *The Conquering Power*, based on Balzac's novel, *Eugenie Grandet*. Released in the summer of 1921, *The Conquering Power* featured Alice in the novel's title role, with Rudolph Valentino as her cousin, Charles. It is worthwhile noting that on prints of the film, Alice receives the only star billing above the title. *The Conquering Power* was the last film in which Miss Terry and Valentino appeared together.

Ingram followed these two sophisticated, continental productions with—of all things—a rural stage comedy, *Turn to the Right*. However, his direction, as in his earlier efforts, could not be

Alice Terry as Eugénie Grandet in *The Conquering Power* (1921).

faulted. *Moving Picture World* (January 21, 1922) commented, "It is the exquisite combination of human interest and comedy, the blending in fact, of all the tried and proven elements essential to the success of drama that gives Rex Ingram's *Turn to the Right* the flattering distinction of being the photographed parallel to the great stage success." Alice, as Elsie Tillinger, was featured with a new leading man, Jack Mulhall.

The Prisoner of Zenda, again directed by Ingram, and released in July 1922, had Alice cast as Princess Flavia, a role to which she brought a serenity and a regality that few actresses at that time, or any other, could match. Regrettably, the production does not live up to the acting of Miss Terry or the other leading players—Lewis Stone,

Barbara La Marr, and Stuart Holmes—it is dull and overloaded with titles. The film introduced a Rex Ingram discovery, Ramon Samaniegos, in the role of Rupert of Hentzau. As Ramon Novarro, Samaniegos was destined for stardom. He would be Miss Terry's leading man in many future films, and as far as Alice is concerned he was the finest actor with whom she worked.

Shortly after completion of *The Prisoner of Zenda,* Alice Terry and Rex Ingram were married. "No Romeo or Juliet of your imagination could be more physically attractive or mentally alluring than these two," wrote Barbara Beach in *Motion Picture Magazine* (January 1922). "Rex is twenty-seven or twenty-eight, as attractive as any matinee idol. Alice Terry is as lovely to look upon

Alice Terry and Ramon Novarro, photographed by Clarence Sinclair Bull.

Alice Terry, as Aline de Kercadiou in *Scaramouche*
(1923).

as the bride of your heart was on the day you loved her best. She is untouched by that modernity which is turning, not only movie girls but society girls, into the cigaret smoking neurasthenics so aptly described by F. Scott Fitzgerald.''

Two features, directed by Ingram, and with Ramon Novarro as Alice's leading man, were released in 1923. In March came *Where the Pavement Ends,* a tale of love and missionary work in the South Sea islands. *Scaramouche,* based on the popular, if trashy, novel by Rafael Sabatini, followed. Both features added to the popular and critical appeal of the Ingrams.

In 1924, Alice and Rex settled on the French Riviera. Ingram was tired of the Hollywood studio system, and longed for a studio of his own, at which he could work at a leisurely pace. The Victorine Studios in Nice proved an ideal work place, with the Mediterranean beaches never too far

Lewis Stone, Alice Terry, and John Bowers in *Confessions of a Queen* (1925).

Alice Terry, as Freya Talberg, prepares to meet her death in *Mare Nostrum* (1926).

away. The first Ingram production shot in Europe, and in North Africa, was *The Arab*, starring Alice Terry and Ramon Novarro. With cinema audiences already bored by the never-ending follow-ups to Valentino's 1921 vehicle *The Sheik,* it was not a huge success. Ingram was not concerned.

For the first time in four years, Alice Terry worked with a director other than her husband. Her 1925 releases were directed by Reginald Barker (*The Great Divide*), Victor Seastrom (*Confessions of a Queen*), and Henry King (*Sackcloth and Scarlet* and *Any Woman*).

Alice was back in Europe under Rex Ingram's direction for her two 1926 features, *Mare Nostrum* and *The Magician*. The latter, based on an early Somerset Maugham novel, is chiefly remembered for its exotic opening sequence, and its use of two great continental actors, Paul Wegener and Ivan Petrovich, to support Miss Terry.

Mare Nostrum, from a novel by Vicente Blasco-Ibanez, is Alice's personal favorite. She considers it the only film in which she was given a real opportunity to act. Certainly, critics at the time agreed with her. After its opening at New York's Criterion Theatre, *Moving Picture World* (February 27, 1926) commented, "Alice Terry, always beautiful, never looked more stunning than as Freya, and superbly handles this role. Aided by Mr. Ingram's excellent direction she makes this character a continual enigma. There is a strange fascination surrounding this woman; you are

Alice Terry and Ivan Petrovich (right) in *The Garden of Allah* (1927).

never quite sure as to whether she is the goddess personified or merely her physical counterpart, her attitude at times suggests first one and then the other."

Ramon Novarro and Alice Terry were reunited for *Lovers?*, directed by John M. Stahl, released in April 1927. Then came Alice's last screen appearance in *The Garden of Allah,* playing Domini to Ivan Petrovich's Boris. Sadly, her final screen appearance was not too well received. *Moving Picture World* (September 10, 1927) wrote, "Ivan Petrovich never becomes either Boris or Father Adrian, and Domini is merely the beautiful but chill Alice Terry, charming in her quieter moments, but unable to rise to the real position of the unmasking."

The Garden of Allah was an independent production, only released by M-G-M, who had found Rex Ingram too difficult to handle. Alice seemed content to retire from screen acting without a murmur of protest or regret. One story had it that she was beginning to put on weight, and was advised to either give up candy or give up movies.

Alice and Rex continued to live in Europe, with Rex concentrating on his painting and sculpture. In 1931, he directed and starred in *Baroud,* a tale of Arab life and love, for which he had a particular fascination. Alice worked as his co-director on the production. It was not the first occasion; many times in the past when he had felt out of sorts, she had taken over the direction.

Baroud was released in the States in 1933 as

Antonio Moreno and Alice Terry in *Mare Nostrum* (1926).

Love in Morocco by Ideal Films. Commented the *New York Times* (March 20, 1933), "It is an unusual entertainment, pleasantly amateurish in its acting, juvenile in its story development and definitely charming in its recreation of the Moroccan atmosphere and the dark beauty of its people as idealized by Mr. Ingram's cameras."

The Ingrams returned to the States prior to the outbreak of the Second World War, and settled in North Hollywood in company with Alice's sister, Edna, and her husband. Alice was at Rex's bedside when he died on July 22, 1950. Today, this fine actress, who never really cared about her film career, lives in seclusion with her sister in the house that she and Rex bought in the thirties.

PART IV.

The Fan Magazines:
Their Stories and Their Writers

13

The Fan Magazines

"*We were contemplating a* precarious new institution that was looked down upon as the unwanted step-child of the arts. And it was pleasant being a pioneer guardian of so wistful and battered a young medium of expression." So wrote Richard Watts, Jr., in the New York *Herald Tribune* of September 16, 1940, looking back to the silent days when he had been the distinguished film critic for that equally distinguished newspaper.

To have been a film critic or fan magazine writer during the silent era must have been both exciting and fun. So much was happening in the film industry: so many innovations; so many new celebrities, and also so many film magazines and writers to record those happenings. In the States, *Photoplay* reigned as King, but its leadership was constantly being challenged by *Motion Picture Magazine, Motion Picture Classic, Movie Weekly,* and *Picture Play.*

Pictures and Picturegoer was Britain's leading film magazine, and it had only one competitor, *Picture Show.* Although in the late twenties the very superior, one might almost say intellectual, *Film Weekly* began publication, but it was only to be swallowed up by *Picturegoer*—to give it its shorter and better-known title—at the outbreak of the Second World War.

Photoplay began publication in 1911, under the managing editorship of Neil G. Caward. Caward was succeeded in 1913 by R. S. Hanford, and, then, with the January 1915, issue, James R. Quirk became vice-president of the Photoplay Publishing Company.

James R. Quirk* was to guide *Photoplay* until his death in Hollywood on August 1, 1932, at the age of forty seven. He built up *Photoplay* to be the finest film magazine of all time. Serious film criticism may be said to have begun with the introduction of Julian Johnson's "Department of Comment and Criticism on Current Photoplays" in the November 1915 issue. In 1920 the distinguished critic Burns Mantle began reviewing films for *Photoplay.* In the same year, Quirk introduced the Photoplay Gold Medals, the first award going to Frank Borzage's *Humoresque.* Adela Rogers St.

*For detailed information on James R. Quirk and *Photoplay,* see "Quirk of Photoplay" by Lawrence J. Quirk in *Films in Review* (March 1955) and *The Talkies* foreword by Lawrence J. Quirk, introduction by Richard Griffith (*Dover Publications* 1971). One of the few recent interviews with Mrs. St. Johns is by Sandra Shevey in the January 1974 issue of *Playgirl.*

Johns was possibly the most influential writer on the film industry, and she was a regular columnist for *Photoplay*.

Tailing just behind *Photoplay* in terms of both quality and popularity was *Motion Picture Magazine,* founded in February 1911 by J. Stuart Blackton and Eugene V. Brewster as *Motion Picture Story Magazine*. (The title was changed with the issue of March 1914.)

Motion Picture Story Magazine was established originally as a publicity organ for the companies comprising the Motion Picture Patents group; J. Stuart Blackton was vice-president of one of the member companies, Vitagraph. The magazine was to publish fictionalized versions of the film releases of the various companies, with each company being allotted equal space.

Gradually, the stock in the publishing company was bought up by Brewster until he eventually not only controlled the magazine, but was also able to launch further publications, notably *Motion Picture Classic, Shadowland,* and *Movie Weekly*. Eugene V. Brewster was quite a remarkable man. Born at Bay Shore, Long Island, on September 7, 1871, he attended Pennington Seminary and Princeton University. In 1906 he published *What To Do with Trusts,* and by the twenties, aside from his film magazines, was publishing biographies of Woodrow Wilson and Napoleon, together with books on art, the theater and finance. He esti-

mated his wealth at three million dollars.

By the late twenties, Brewster had lost control of his empire and was in California, trying to promote his third wife, Corliss Palmer, into a star. He failed, and in August 1931 filed petition for bankruptcy, curiously enough within ten days of his one-time partner, J. Stuart Blackton's filing a similar petition. Eugene V. Brewster died in Brooklyn on January 1, 1939.

Motion Picture Magazine had its team of special writers, in particular Adele Whitely Fletcher, Gladys Hall, and Hazel Simpson Naylor. It must have been the only magazine to admit that many of its contributors also wrote for the periodical under pseudonyms. In the issue of December 1917, it announced that Lillian May was also Lillian Montanye, that Roberta Courtlandt was Pearl Gaddis, and that Peter Wade was really Edwin M. LaRoche.

The fan magazines, as they were once known and once so highly regarded, are gone. The majority of their writers have likewise disappeared, Frederick James Smith, Leonard Hall, Harry Carr, and Harriette Underhill are no more. Their work, however, like that of the filmmakers of whom they once wrote, lives on. As long as there are students and scholars researching the cinema's silent era, the early fan magazines and their writers will never be forgotten.

14

*Adele Whitely Fletcher**

Adele Whitely Fletcher's first contact with the film industry came in 1916, when she went to work for Vitagraph's publicity department. Some of her first articles appeared in the long-forgotten *Photo-Play Journal,* which, interestingly, published the first writings of Edward Wagenknecht. Miss Fletcher became editor of *Motion Picture Magazine,* with the issue of February 1920, and for that periodical wrote the popular "We Interview" series with Gladys Hall. Since that time, Miss Fletcher has contributed pieces to, and edited, many film magazines, including *Movie Weekly* and *Photoplay.* She lives in New York, and still contributes articles to *Modern Screen* et al.

"AS   You started with Vitagraph around 1916, I believe?

AWF   I did. I went down there. I had to leave school and go to work, and my family got me a job in the Metropolitan Life Insurance Company. Well, at the end of the first week I used to wish that the elevated structure that the subway went on to

*This interview was first published, in a slightly different format, in *Film Fan Monthly* (February 1974). Copyright © 1974 *Film Fan Monthly.*

Adele Whitely Fletcher.

take me home would collapse, and it would be all over. Finally I was offered a job as secretary to the director of publicity at the old Vitagraph studios, which were not far from where we lived in Flatbush. My grandfather and great-grandfather were theatre people, and my mother had a horror of the theatre. It was feast or famine in her mind. It was incomprehensible to her that I would give up a nice, safe, decent job with a life insurance company, and go and work for the Vitagraph studio. I think she just thought the mark of Cain was on me, and there wasn't much that she could do about it.

Anyway, I loved it. Sam Spedon (Vitagraph's head of publicity) was a rough character, not rough in the sense of ill-bred, but tough, and he said this woman's magazine was very interested in a fashion story, and nobody in the department had been able to do it. These men were newspaper men. They didn't know anything about women's clothes. So, for two or three days, I would eat a sandwich at my desk for lunch, and I did fashion stories, rifling through all the fashion magazines that were available. I put them on Mr. Spedon's desk, and I don't think I've ever known such anxiety or nervousness as waiting for him to pick them up and read them. He said, 'Who wrote this?' I said, 'I did, Mr. Spedon,' and he said 'What the hell are you doing as a stenographer in this department? From now on, you're a writer.' And he raised me $15 a week. I couldn't wait to get home and tell my mother I had done right to go to the Vitagraph studio.

AS What were some of the first stories that you wrote?

AWF You've heard of Anita Stewart? I wrote her 'Talks to Girls.' When I think about it now, I die.

AS From Vitagraph, you went, I believe to Brewster Publications?

AWF I edited *Motion Picture Magazine*. Then I was made editorial director of all the Brewster Publications. When I first went to *Motion Picture Magazine*, Frederick James Smith was editor-in-chief. Then he got very interested in *Shadowland*, and Fred thought he was going to break away from *Motion Picture* with it.

AS Were you involved with the 'Fame and Fortune' contests that Eugene Brewster used to run?

AWF Clara Bow was one of our winners, and Mary Astor. I have always thought that was Mr. Brewster's ploy to bring a lot of attractive girls into the office. I must say he had something to do

with the final choice, but you had to investigate these people. You couldn't let anyone win; you didn't know who they were.

Now, Clara Bow's background was horrendous. Her father used to come into the office, and he was practically illiterate. He would smoke the most foul-smelling cigars, and they were always down to nothing when he came in. He was determined that nothing was going to happen to his little rosebud, and that she was going to get all that was coming to her. And her mother was a really crazy woman. I understand she went for Clara once with a carving knife. Well, if you had any sensitivity at all, you were horrified at taking this girl, who was obviously going to win because she photographed like a dream, and throw her to the wolves. I did my best to let her see New York; let her see good places, take her to good plays. I never tried harder in my life to prepare Clara for what was ahead of her. I took her to the Waldorf—the old Waldorf on Fifth Avenue—for lunch, and Clara didn't know what to eat. Her Coney Island background dictated lobster salad as a very elegant thing. Well, she looked at the capers around the edge of the dish, and she must have thought it was some sort of vermin with which she was not yet familiar, because she said, 'Ugh,' and pushed them away with her fork. She was horrified. I can still see that vulnerable, ambitious and driven, and, in a way, sensitive, little figure sitting there.

AS Wasn't Madame Olga Petrova one of the judges of the contest?

AWF I wouldn't say she was involved. She was often there. Now there is a really great woman. She had such drive. I really love Madame; I really do. She and her late husband Lewis Willoughby, used to come and visit us. I had a daughter, who must have been then nine, and she has never forgotten Petrova. She says today she was the most beautiful woman she ever saw in her life.

I was always very fond of Gloria Swanson, and I must say Mary Pickford and Douglas Fairbanks were a highlight in my life. When they'd get to New York, after they'd been travelling, Mary would always get a cold, and what she did was to go to bed so she'd build up some energy. I'd go up and see her, and Douglas would be climbing up the door, showing me some new muscle flex or something. I think when Douglas left her, something very vital went out of her. I think she was never the same again.

AS Did any of the stars at that time resent your

writing about them?

AWF No, stars at that time were very eager — not this breed of stars. Mae Murray was very difficult. I did a review of one of her films—I can't think which one it was—but she wrote to Eugene Brewster insisting that I be fired. I was not to be allowed to keep on this way! Corinne Griffith, I knew very well, still do.

AS Is it true that she now claims not to be Corinne Griffith, the star of silent films?

AWF She says her sister was Corinne Griffith, and she died, and that because she was a money-maker, Corinne stepped in. It could be true. I don't know that it isn't true, but I know the Corinne Griffith, who was a very young woman at the Vitagraph studios, and was married to Webster Campbell, is the same Corinne Griffith that I know today. She remembers Vitagraph. Webster Campbell was like so many men who married a star. It satisfies their egos to marry the star, and they can't take it. When Corinne wasn't at the studios, he used to entertain extra girls in Corinne's dressing room. We became close friends because I knew about it, and never told her. She always knew I knew it, and confronted me with it, and from that time on we were very good friends.

AS Which person most impressed you during the silent era?

AWF Theda Bara. She was one of the best informed women that I have ever known. She knew who she was. She was Theodosia Goodman. I think she started my interest in food. She would pick me up in her chauffeur-driven car, and we would go to a place in Jersey where they served beautiful Italian food, then we went to a place out on Long Island, where they did beautiful seafood. Always we'd stop along the road to wherever we were going, and the chauffeur would take out a silver cocktail shaker and we'd have a martini, or maybe one-and-a-half martinis, just enough to whet the appetite, and then we'd go and have our lunch.

AS Did you write for *Photoplay* while James Quirk was alive?

AWF I wrote for Quirk. I loved him. He was a real ripsnorting Irish whiskey-drinking Irishman. You could always tell if he liked what you came in with, because if he did, he'd bring this bottle out of the lower desk drawer, and you would have a snort with him before you left. I had an idea once for a series, 'Beauty, Brains or Luck?' I did it again for *Photoplay* not so long ago. If you can get a gimmick like that, it's amazing the material it evokes that you'll get no other way. Now, I'm doing this series for *Modern Screen* called 'The Tales Their Houses Tell,' and things come out that you'd never get in an interview. I've done Henry Fonda, Doris Day, Sandra Dee, Burt Reynolds, Joan Crawford and Mike Douglas. If you get an idea like that, then you can't fail. However dull the person is you can get something from them—and God knows today they're pretty dull, and deliberately antagonistic and difficult.

AS Tell me how you gave Joan Crawford her name?

AWF I was the editor of *Movie Weekly,* and there was a Winter Garden showgirl, Lucille LeSeur. Harry Rapf of Metro was very interested in her, and he offered a five hundred dollar prize for a name. He had very prestigious judges—oh my—but when it came time to judge they were all very busy, and some of them were not available, and they said to me, go ahead, any name you choose is all right with us. And Joan hated the name at first, hated it.

AS You mention being editor of *Movie Weekly,* which reminds me that much later, you were to become editor of *Photoplay.*

AWF I was editor of *Photoplay* for some years. I re-established the *Photoplay* Gold Medal Awards. We had to do something to remove us from all of the other magazines. I must say the Gold Medals were brought out of hiding on a very grand scale. Gallop Polls made the decisions. I left *Photoplay* to become woman's editor of *The American Weekly,* that must have been about nineteen years ago. That was probably the most enriching experience of my life. That's when I ghosted everything Elsa Maxwell did, first in *Photoplay,* and then in *The American Weekly.*

AS Does it depress you to see the way *Photoplay* has deteriorated through the years?

AWF I couldn't not get depressed. I think when I edited *Photoplay*—maybe this is wishful thinking—it was a young woman's magazine. We had fashion; we had Claudette Colbert doing an advice column; we had personalities; we had millions in circulation. I deplore what is said in motion picture magazines today, let me make that firm, but I can't conscientiously be critical of the editors, because I don't know what in hell they could do. If you don't have personalities with whom your readers have enough identification then you have to be shocking. The people in Hollywood who scream about what motion picture magazines are doing should look to themselves. They are using shock to get readers just as Hollywood is using shock to get audiences. I don't say you don't have to modernize your thinking, of course, but I think they're both wrong.''

15

*Ruth Waterbury**

Ruth Waterbury has been associated with *Photoplay* for fifty years, as both a regular contributor and as editor. "Wedded and Parted," which was possibly her first piece for *Photoplay,* appeared in the issue of December 1922. Aside from her magazine and newspaper writing, Miss Waterbury has authored two books: *Elizabeth Taylor* (Appleton-Century, 1964) and *Richard Burton* (Pyramid Books, 1964). This interview took place in Miss Waterbury's Los Angeles home.

"AS   How and why did you become a writer?
RW   I went into journalism, I think, because of my father. I was an only child of very mature parents. My mother was punishing me for something or other—I don't remember what—and my father said, 'Why are you punishing her?' She said, 'Because she lied to me.' And my father said, 'Don't you know she is a natural-born liar? When she grows up, she'll have to be a writer.' Well, this stuck in my mind very definitely; it really did. When I got out of school, both of my parents were

dead, and I was very much alone, and so I began writing.

I was so lonely—this was in New York—and I had a tacky little room. I used to go around and just talk to people to escape my loneliness. Then I wrote some short stories, and I'll never know how it happened, because I didn't know anybody, and I had no money, and I wasn't anybody. But I went to a cocktail party, where there was a literary agent, and I went over, and I said that I had this story. She said, 'Well, I'd like to look at it'; and I got fifty dollars for it. Then they phoned me up from this magazine, and they said they'd like me to write a story a month for them. Well, jeepers! But that wasn't enough for me. I wanted to be on a newspaper, because I thought if I went on a newspaper, then I would learn how to write.

So, I went to this woman, whose name was Flora Mae Holly, and asked her how I could get to be seen in a newspaper. She said, 'Oh, I can fix it up. The City Editor of the *New York World* is a friend of mine, and I'll call him and ask him if he'll see you.' So, I went to see him, and he said to me—of course, today I'd be very diplomatic and polite about it, but then I didn't know enough to be—'What part of the *New York World* do you read? 'Oh,' I said, 'I never read it.' And he said, 'You don't? Why not?' I said, 'Because there's nothing in it to interest a girl.' He said, 'Well, what do you think would interest a girl?' And I said, 'Well, I don't know, but there's a lady lives near to where I live, and she runs a thing called Suzanna Bell's Cat Shop, and she got offered a thousand dollars for her main cat, but she wouldn't take it because she loved that cat so much. Now that's the kind of a story a girl likes to read.' He kind of looked at me, and said, 'What other stories do you know?' So I mentioned three, which I had got through just wanting to talk to somebody. He said, 'If you write them, and I like them, I'll give you thirty-five dollars apiece.' I went right back up on the subway, climbed into my typewriter, wrote all three of them, and came right back down. Of course, I'd been rather well brought up, so I sent my calling card in, and he came out laughing, and I said, 'Here are the stories.' He just looked at me....Subsequently, I got a job on the paper.

AS   How did you first come to write about films?

RW   I was scared every minute of my existence, because I didn't know anything, and one day the city desk called me, and said I was to go to the Waldorf Astoria and interview Rudolph Valentino. Well! The Waldorf Astoria was the most elegant hotel there was—I'd never dare go into it, let alone interview. And I didn't know who Rudolph Valentino was! So, the City Editor said, 'Go up there, and get his story,' and as I turned away from his desk Karl Kitchen, a star reporter, was looking at me, and grinning. He said, 'Listen, Kid, don't bother with that. I've been up there, three of the other reporters have been up there. You can't get to see him. He won't see anybody. Go out and take a walk, and come back and say he wouldn't do it.' Well, I hadn't been brought up on that ethic.

You call the place where they keep the clippings in newspapers the morgue, so I decided to go into the morgue, and see who this Rudolph Valentino was; why they wanted a story on him anyway. So I began to read, and I noticed the address of his lawyer there. Now, at that time, Valentino was having a quarrel with Famous Players, who had his contract. My father had been a lawyer, so I thought I would go and see his lawyer. I talked to his lawyer, George Gordon Bottle, on the phone, and I said, 'I beg your pardon, but you're losing your client's case in the papers. Famous Players is

in every day, and he's not saying anything. I would like to put his case in front of the people.' He said, 'I haven't met a reporter I trust.' I said, 'I don't know why you couldn't trust me if I'm right in front of you, write the story, and phone the story in before you.' He said, 'Would you do that?' I said, 'Yes, sir, I would.' So, in half-an-hour, he produced Valentino, and Valentino just talked his heart out.

Well, the next morning every damned newspaper in New York was calling me, because he was so red hot. Then Rudy decided he wouldn't let anybody talk to him but me, and *Metropolitan,* which was an important magazine, called me, and offered me eight hundred dollars to do a Valentino story. I tell you, you can't know unless you've been a poor boy where every quarter, every dime is important, to be suddenty offered eight hundred dollars, you'd take your head off, and hand it to them. Then Jim Quirk, who was the editor of *Photoplay,* went after me, and he offered me one hundred and twenty-five dollars a week. I didn't know what to do; I went back to the *World,* and I asked Karl Kitchen. He said, 'Don't be a fool; take it. You'll never get it out of us, but Quirk never keeps anybody. He gets people, and then he fires them, so be prepared that it probably won't last more than a month.'

AS   What type of man was Quirk?

RW   He was a very amazing man; he was a very colorful man. He was a kind man, and witty, and so sophisticated, which, heaven knows, his correspondent was not. But he was forever firing people. He did have an impulse to fire people. I can't tell you the number of days I would come into the office in the morning and everybody would have been let out, the telephone girls, the file clerks, everybody. And there we'd be. There'd be nobody to answer the phones, there'd be nobody to do anything. He called me Snip, and he'd say, 'Oh Snip, I didn't mean to do it,' and I'd say, 'Jim, how are we going to get this magazine out? There, you've done it again. Now will you quit?' But I amused him. I think that was my hold on him. He just thought I was kinda funny. I stayed with Jim almost to the end of his life, not quite, because by that time I was getting other offers. I don't know, I have some sort of trashy appeal in my writing. I say this in absolute sincerity. I don't know what it is. I am not a stylish writer, but I have a public.

AS Was Quirk interested in films, or was *Photoplay* purely a business venture?

RW Oh, he was very interested in films. He was a very bright man, but he would do impossible things. I got married at the big, fast age of eighteen, and, of course, I was fixated with my career. I was very amused by Jim, and he was very amused by me. One day, he came and said, 'What are you doing?' I said, 'I'm thinking.' He said, 'Think at home.' He half meant it too; he wanted me pounding at that typewriter.

Of course, my poor husband! Jim would call you in the middle of the night, and say 'Snip, if we did this on page 34 instead of page 35, would you mind coming up here?' Your husband doesn't know why you're piling out at three o'clock in the morning to do something he forgot about all that while. I invented—I truly invented—the phrase 'Going Hollywood.' This was entirely Jim's fault. He had actually invented the phrase, and he sent the covers through to the printers in Chicago with this line. Then he didn't know what it meant! He got me at four o'clock in the morning, and said, 'Snip, we're in trouble. For God's sake get up here.' So, of course, I had to stop and have the quarrel with my husband first. On the way, I saw the morning papers on the newsstands, and there was a headline, 'Dolores Del Rio and Husband Separate.' I said, 'That's what it is; that's Going Hollywood.' I wrote the story, and we phoned it to Chicago at six o'clock in the morning. This was the way Jim was. You had to be able to adjust to that crazy temperament.

AS You took over as editor of *Photoplay* in 1935. Who took over when Quirk died?

RW Actually, it was edited—technically—by Kathryn Dougherty, who was the general bookkeeper. She took it over; then a man named Frederick James Smith. Of course, Kathryn Dougherty was in a terrible spot. She was a rather pretty thing, and, of course, she didn't like me. Now, I assure you there was never anything romantic between Jim and me. We were just wonderful friends, and we had a wonderful time together. In a peculiar way we understood one another. But K.D. hated me. I was in her way. She just detested me. So many people think there's no trick to writing. What do you do? Just write. When you edit, you just edit. She was that kind. Well, all the magazine did for about two years, when she took over, was dive, dive, dive. In the meantime, I

was offered this thing at *Silver Screen;* I created the newsstand issue of *Silver Screen.* I said, 'Look, there's no such thing as a ten cent motion picture magazine on the newsstands.' The depression was on which conditioned everything, but we sold like mad, because we were only ten cents. Then *Photoplay* was bought by McFadden Publications, which was a very smart operation. Of course, Kathryn Dougherty came with the magazine, but they didn't have her up there more than twenty minutes. I don't know whatever became of her. I went in as editor, and stayed as editor.

AS Did Bernarr McFadden interfere at all in the editing of the magazine?

RW Oh no. The trouble with him was he was a very erotic old man. You had to keep out of his way. He was a personality. After all, this was a man who had no background, no breeding, nothing, who made himself a multi-multi-multi millionaire. He was the worst lecher that ever lived. God, he was a dreadful old man. He'd have some girl pull out a file, and it was always very crowded, so the girl would be bending down, and he'd brush against her. He hated girls to wear lipstick, so when I had to see him, I'd put on more lipstick than you ever saw. He got a little discouraged with me. He was just awful, but he had a formula—he sure as hell did. We always kept it as a class magazine until this war. They could have kept it there. I used to have to take the covers up to show the old man, and I remember once he said, 'Why can't I have one with a girl whose butt is showing?' This was his standard.

AS You had overall control of the magazine?

RW Oh yes. Pardon my conceit, but I did something that was very daring. I remember one issue, I put the Academy Award winners in before they were announced. It was so clear who was going to win, so we had them on the covers.

I got a painting made of Gable before they made a decision of *Gone with the Wind.* I knew they had to have Gable, I knew they couldn't take anyone else. I changed the kind of cover we used too, and the first one I used on that was Shirley Temple, and we picked up 80,000 circulation on that issue. They don't have that kind of daring now. Every month, you put on Patty Duke. Do you think there are that many people interested in Patty Duke? None of the people they are bringing in are stars, they haven't got that quality, and so, therefore, you can't expect the magazines to sell.

AS   Why did you leave *Photoplay?*

RW   I had had a lot of offers from out here (Los Angeles), and in the meantime my husband had died. Louella Parsons had been after me for some time to come and work for her, and I thought, 'I think what I want to do is pull up stakes from New York and go to California, and this is a perfectly good entrée.' I enjoyed working with Louella, but you couldn't do quite the same as you, yourself, would have done; you were secondary.

AS   When do you think the decline of *Photoplay* set in?

RW   I think, perhaps, some of it was the war. The most important stars did go to war. For instance, Gable, during the war, discovered he wasn't a young man. People like Jimmie Stewart, who was relatively young, came in, but it never quite caught back where it was before the war, like many things. The whole world changed after the war. The great producers, they had become a lot older. I think a lot of the pornography today; it's a matter of age. I think there's a lot of nasty old men sitting around putting that pornography out, because they're not stimulated by the average relationship anymore. I think it's too bad, because we were the greatest image in the world. I don't think the image could be presented now as any too good. How can you tell if people would want drugs so much today, if we still gave them this dream world on film? I don't know where the decay begins in anything. I love Hollywood, I love its people. I always will. But, of course, the Hollywood that went up to 1940 is a very different Hollywood from this Hollywood of 1972.

AS   Who would you say were the most fascinating personalities that you met in each decade?

RW   Well, of course, I met Ronald Colman. Valentino was an extremely handsome man, but Colman was handsome in a different way. Physical beauty of the males in Hollywood at that time was really a thing. I know the first time I went to Malibu, I was invited down by Neil Hamilton, and all of a sudden I fainted dead away. It was just Joel McCrea walking down the beach. I'd never seen anything like that! Really the ugliness in pictures today is something awful. There were none of those drab-looking people like Dustin Hoffman — can you believe any girl looks at Dustin Hoffman and gets a thrill? I can't.

AS   But don't you feel in the Twenties that male charm was purely effeminate?

RW   I don't agree with that. I think Valentino was scared, he was a pretty simple Italian, and of course, he was dominated by that dreadful woman, Rambova. Gable, I think, was the man of the Thirties, definitely. Of course, there's nothing the matter with John Wayne to this day. I don't know who came in the Forties.

AS   The Forties were in a way the dead years, the Victor Mature era.

RW   Up in the Parsons' office, Dorothy Manners, Louella and myself, we all hated Victor Mature, and Louella said to me, 'Ruthie?' and I said, 'To hell, fire me. I'm not going to interview Victor Mature.' He could never get in the paper.

AS   Who was the most exciting personality that you met?

RW   Clark Gable.

AS   Why?

RW   He was a man, a real man. Believe me.

AS   Can I ask you something about your fellow writers?

RW   You mean, did I like them?

AS   How do you see yourself in comparison with them?

RW   I think this is a matter of fluke that some of us got established on the newspaper side, and stayed on the newspaper side. Adela Rogers St. Johns is a working newspaperwoman, a working writer. She knows the score, and I think she's very, very capable and clever. I admire her very much. I don't know whether I should say this, but I think it is very rude to have had a love affair with an important man, like Scott Fitzgerald and then write a piece about him. What a mess he was at the end of his life! I just don't think you do such things, I really don't.

Of course, I was very fond of Louella Parsons. You just can't help being fond of Louella. Hedda Hopper never wrote. She had two or three writers working for her. She would go around, getting the stuff, but she couldn't write at all. Couldn't write her name!

AS   Generally speaking, has the film industry destroyed people such as yourself?

RW   I can get to almost anybody, but also I don't have to get to anybody. I have made enough money, and I can live as I want to live. So I will not take any backtalk from any little punks who say, 'I don't talk to people like you.' I say, 'Great, good,' and walk out."

Checklists

The following checklists should in no way be considered definitive. They are intended to provide a thorough reading list of articles and books on one hundred silent stars.

It should, of course, be remembered that articles signed by stars, and included in this listing, were seldom if ever actually written by them.

Renée Adorée

Albert, Katherine. "A Daughter of the Sawdust." *Screenland* (December 1927).
———. "The Girl Who Just Missed Stardom." *Photoplay* (June 1926).
Uselton, Roi A. "Renée Adorée." *Films in Review* (June-July 1968). *See also* issue of August-September 1968.
Wilson, Henry. "The Genius Enchanting." *Photoplay* (June 1926).
Anonymous. "Renée Adorée; The Girl on the Cover." *Pictures and Picturegoer* (January 1930).

Mignon Anderson

Anderson, Mignon. "Flirting with the Undertaker." *Photoplay* (June 1914).

Renée Adorée and Harry Carey in a rare still of their unproduced version of *Rose-Marie*. It was subsequently produced starring Joan Crawford, and released in 1928.

Holmes, Harriet. "Winsome Mignon Anderson." *Photoplay* (November 1913).

Anonymous. "Brief Biographies of Popular Players." *Motion Picture Magazine* (October 1915).

————. "Mignon Anderson's Career." *Moving Picture Stories* (June 29, 1917).

Vilma Banky

Biery, Ruth. "Companionate Stardom." *Photoplay* (March 1928).

Chute, Margaret. "With Vilma Banky on Location." *Pictures and Picturegoer* (May 1929).

Howe, Herbert. "Hot Dickety-Dog." *Photoplay* (December 1925).

Kenworthy, Mildred. "Marry? I Zink Ya." *Photoplay* (April 1927).

West, Myrtle. "The Price They Paid for Stardom." *Photoplay* (November 1926).

York, Cal. "The Girl on the Cover." *Photoplay* (April 1926).

Anonymous. "A Beautiful Blonde." *Pictures and Picturegoer* (November 1926).

Theda Bara

Bara, Pauline. "My Theda Bara II." *Motion Picture Classic* (January 1921).

Bara, Theda. "How I Became a Vampire." *Forum* (June-July 1919).

Bodeen, DeWitt. "Theda Bara." *Films in Review* (May 1968). *See also* issue of August-September 1968.

Courtlandt, Roberta. "The Divine Theda." *Motion Picture Magazine* (April 1917).

Evans, Delight. "Does Theda Bara Believe Her Own Press Agent?" *Photoplay* (May 1918).

Franklin, Wallace. "Purgatory's Ivory Angel." *Photoplay* (September 1915).

Theda Bara, with her director, J. Gordon Edwards and his son (circa 1917).

Vilma Banky.

Hall, Gladys, and Fletcher, Adele Whitely. "We Interview Theda Bara." *Motion Picture Magazine* (November 1922).

McKelvie, Martha Groves. "O-o-o-o Theda!" *Motion Picture Classic* (September 1918).

Petrova, Olga. "Mme. Petrova Interviews Theda Bara." *Shadowland* (March-April 1920).

Smith, Agnes. "The Confessions of Theda Bara." *Photoplay* (June 1920).

Smith, Frederick James. "Keeping an Appointment with Theda Bara." *Motion Picture Classic* (February 1919).

Anonymous. "Theda Bara's Defense." *Motion Picture Magazine* (August 1916).

———. "Cleopatra Plays a Return Date." *Photoplay* (October 1917).

———. "Come Home—All Is Forgiven." *Photoplay* (February 1923).

———. "Should Old Acquaintance Be Forgot?" *Photoplay* (August 1929).

Richard Barthelmess

Barrett, E.E. "Dick's Different." *Pictures and Picturegoer* (December 1926).

Barthelmess, Richard. "A La William Tell." *Photo-Play Journal* (June 1919).

———. "Fifteen Years of Film Fame." *Pictures and Picturegoer* (June 10, 1933).

Brewster, Eleanor. "When Fan Meets Favorite." *Motion Picture Magazine* (June 1918).

Collier, Lionel. "The Idol Richard." *Pictures and Picturegoer* (June 1929).

Denton, Frances. "Dick's New Contract." *Photoplay* (September 1920).

Elliot, John Addison. "Honeymoon Cottage." *Picture Play* (November 1920).

Evans, Delight. "A Wealthy Manufacturer's Son." *Photoplay* (September 1919).

Hall, Alice. "A Nice Boy Barthelmess." *Pictures and Picturegoer* (October 1921).

Hall, Gladys. "Richard the Tenth." *Motion Picture Magazine* (April 1921).

Howe, Herbert. "Call Mr. Ponce de Leon." *Photoplay* (April 1918).

———. "The Real Dick Barthelmess." *Picture Play* (August 1920).

Knight, Burt. "What Mrs. Barthelmess Thinks of Richard." *Cinema Art* (April 1926).

Levenson, Lewis F. "A Matter-of-Fact Young Man." *Photoplay Journal* (May 1921).

MacLaurin, Dane. "Casualties Survived." *Photo-Play Journal* (March 1918).

Naylor, Hazel Simpson. "Richard Barthelmess—An

Richard Barthelmess, as The Yellow Man, in *Broken Blossoms* (1919).

Impression." *Motion Picture Magazine* (February 1920).

Service, Faith, "Pre-Griffith Days." *Motion Picture Classic* (December 1922).

Smith, Frederick James. "Barthelmess, the Boy." *Motion Picture Classic* (January 1920).

Spears, Jack. "Richard Barthelmess." *Films in Review* (January 1958).

Taylor, Mary Keane. "And He Wants To Be a Playwright!" *Motion Picture Classic* (February 1919).

Underhill, Harriette. "What They Know about Each Other." *Photoplay* (May 1925).

Walker, Helen Louise. "A Plea for Privacy." *Photoplay* (September 1929).

Weitzel, Edward. "The Rise of Richard Barthelmess." *Moving Picture World* (July 26, 1919).

Wilson, B. F. "A Terribly Intimate Portrait." *Motion Picture Classic* (August 1924).

Woodhouse, Bruce. "The Screen's Young Veteran." *Pictures and Picturegoer* (July 7, 1936).

Anonymous. "Richard's Himself Again." *Talking Screen* (January 1930).

Beverly Bayne.

Beverly Bayne

Craig, Johnstone. "La Fille au Devant." *Photoplay* (October 1915).
Fullbright, Tom. "Presenting Miss Beverly Bayne."

Classic Film Collector (Winter 1970 - Summer 1972).
Howard, Lillian. "Beverly Bayne, a Living Van Dyke." *Photoplay* (March 1927).
Pike, Cameron. "Beverly's Baby Stars." *Photoplay* (May 1918).

Madge Bellamy

Beach, Barbara. "A Lighted Torch." *Motion Picture Classic* (January 1921).

E. E. B. "Mainly about Madge." *Pictures and Picturegoer* (July 1926).

Gebhart, Myrtle. "The Gold Girl." *Motion Picture Magazine* (April 1922).

Jordan, Joan. "Madge Make-Believe." *Photoplay* (March 1921).

Larkin, Mark. "Giving the Men a Break." *Photoplay* (March 1929).

Smith, Agnes. "Peroxide Pep." *Photoplay* (October 1926)

Spensley, Dorothy. "Why 6 Marriages Failed." *Photoplay* (May 1930).

"Madge Bellamy Edition." *Fox Folks* (September 1925).

Betty Blythe

Baremore, R. W. "Betty—Blythe—and Gay." *Photo-Play Journal* (June 1919).

Betty Blythe.

Madge Bellamy.

Blythe, Betty. "On the Golden Stairs." *Picture Play* (August 1920).

———. "What Is Love?" *Photoplay* (November 1924).

Cheatham, Maude S. "Betty Blythe: The Peacock Princess." *Motion Picture Classic* (February 1920).

Fletcher, Adele and Hall, Gladys. "We Interview the Queen of Sheba." *Motion Picture Magazine* (August 1921).

Hall, Gladys. "Betty Blythe Gives Thanks." *Motion Picture Magazine* (December 1918).

Lonergan, Elizabeth. "My Impressions of London." *Pictures and Picturegoer* (September 1924).

Naylor, Hazel Simpson. "Coffee Pots and Crowns." *Motion Picture Magazine* (February 1921).

Patterson, Ada. "When Venus Ordered Hash." *Photoplay* (December 1921).

Rogers St. Johns, Adela. "When the Queen of Sheba Was a Kid." *Photoplay* (January 1921).

Smith, Frederick James. "Betty Goes to Broadway." *Motion Picture Magazine* (August 1921).

Williams, Louise. "Rearranging Memory's Word Box." *Picture Play* (December 1919).

Anonymous. "The Family Name is Blythe." *Photoplay* (September 1918).

Clara Bow.

———. "Star or Shrave, Betty Blythe is No Bolshevik." *Photoplay* (December 1919).
———. "Queen of Sheba Returns To Play Small Part with Garbo." *Pictures and Picturegoer* (September 21, 1935).

Hobart Bosworth

Beach, Barbara. "The Pioneer of the Shadowed Drama." *Motion Picture Magazine* (February 1922).
Belfrage, Cedric. "Mark My Words." *Motion Picture Magazine* (April 1928).
Bosworth, Hobart. "The Picture Forty-Niners." *Photoplay* (February 1915).
Cheatham, Maude S. "Sea Dog Bosworth." *Motion Picture Classic* (December 1919).
Corliss, Allen. "They Both Came Back." *Photoplay* (April 1920).
Anonymous. "Bosworth's Art Analyzed by Critic." *Moving Picture Weekly* (September 18, 1915).

Clara Bow

Alton, Maxine. "Clara's First Train Ride." *Photoplay* (January 1930).
Behlmer, Rudy. "Clara Bow." *Films in Review* (October 1963). *See also* issue of November 1963.
Bow, Clara. "Evoking Emotions Is No Child's Play." *Theatre Magazine* (November 1927).
———. "Quit Pickin' on Me!" *Photoplay* (January 1931).
———. "My Second Career." *Pictures and Picturegoer* (December 3, 1932).
Chaffin, Glenn. "She Rolls Her Own Fat Away." *Photoplay* (June 1925).
Chrisman, J. Eugene. "Clara Chooses Motherhood." *Pictures and Picturegoer* (May 21, 1932).
Fletcher, Adele Whitely. "Beauty, Brains or Luck?" *Photoplay* (September 1930).
Hall, Leonard. "Seeing Clara Bow." *Photoplay* (May 1930).
———. "What about Clara Bow?" *Photoplay* (October 1930).
McVeigh, Blake. "A Comedy of Errors." *Photoplay* (June 1925).
Mortimer, Reg. "Clara Bow." *Pictures and Picturegoer* (October 3, 1931).
Perry, Martin. "Seeing's Believing." *Motion Picture Classic* (September 1922).
Phillips, Malcolm D. "Can Clara Bow Come Back?" *Pictures and Picturegoer* (November 26, 1932).
Pinkley, Virgil. "Clara Bow's Football Heroes." *Pictures and Picturegoer* (February 1930).

Clara Bow and Percy Marmont in *Mantrap* (1926).

R. C. B. "She's It." *Pictures and Picturegoer* (June 6, 1931).
Robinson, David. "The 'It' Girl." *Sight and Sound* (Autumn 1968).
Rogers St. Johns, Adela. "My Life Story." *Photoplay* (February 1928-April 1928).
Shirley, Lois. "Empty Hearted." *Photoplay* (October 1929).
Woodward, Michael. "That Awful 'It'!" *Photoplay* (July 1930).

Evelyn Brent

Albert, Katherine. "She Eats and Tells." *Photoplay* (January 1931).
Biery, Ruth. "Suicide Never Pays." *Photoplay* (May 1928).
Chute, Margaret. "The Brent's Due." *Pictures and Picturegoer* (September 1929).
Moulton, Herbert. "Film Beauty Would Like to Play a Real Hag." *The Pre-View* (September 19, 1923).
Anonymous. "Evelyn Brent Checklist." *Monthly Film Bulletin* (April 1966).

Evelyn Brent.

Gladys Brockwell

Evans, C. D. "G. W. B." *Motion Picture Classic* (October 1917).
Handy, Truman B. "Iconclast." *Motion Picture Classic* (September 1922).
Kingsley, Grace. "Rich Girl, Poor Girl, Beggar Girl—Thief." *Photoplay* (April 1917).
McKelvie, Martha G. "A Glance at Gladys." *Motion Picture Magazine* (June 1919).

Betty Bronson

Clark, Frances. "Say You Believe in Peter Pan." *Photoplay* (March 1927).
Everson, William K. "Betty Bronson." *Film Fan Monthly* (November 1971).
Gebhart, Myrtle. "Peter Pan's Rebellion." *Picture Play* (October 1929).
Rogers St. Johns, Adela. "Betty Bronson—Sub-deb of the Film Set." *Photoplay* (January 1926).

Gladys Brockwell.

A rare shot of Betty Bronson as the Virgin Mary in *Ben-Hur* (1925).

Betty Bronson in *A Kiss for Cinderella* (1926).

John Bunny

Bunny, John. "How It Feels To Be a Comedian." *Photoplay* (October 1914).

Dunham, Harold. "John Bunny." *The Silent Picture* (Winter 1968-1969).

Gill, Sam. "John Bunny Checklist." *The Silent Picture* (Summer 1972).

Lanier, Henry Wyndham. "The Coquelin of the Movies." *World's Work* (March 1915).

Palmer, John. "Mr. Bunny." *Saturday Review* (April 1914).

Pemberton, Ralph Brock. "A Man Seen Daily by Millions." *American Magazine* (August 1914).

Waterbury, Ruth. "The Final Fadeout." *Photoplay* (March 1926).

Anonymous. "Mr. John Bunny." *Moving Picture World* (October 14, 1911).

———. "The Best Known Face in the World." *London Evening News* (April 28, 1915).

———. "The Art of John Bunny." *Bioscope* (May 6, 1915).

———. "Death of John Bunny." *Moving Picture World* (May 8, 1915).

———. "The World's Loss." *Punch* (May 12, 1915).

———. "His Face Was His Fortune." *Pictures and Picturegoer* (May 15, 1915).

———. "John Bunny." *Moving Picture Magazine* (May 1915).

Francis X. Bushman

Biery, Ruth. "What Killed Francis X. Bushman." *Photoplay* (January 1928).

Bushman, Francis X. "From the Inside of the Studio." *Picture-Play Weekly* (April 10, 1915).

———. "A Thrilling Parallel." *Photoplay* (May 1915).

———. "How I Keep My Strength." *Photoplay* (May 1915).

Fisher, Thornton. "Francis X. Bushman—Star." *Moving Picture World* (February 27, 1915).

Geraghty, Tom J. "The Home of the Great Bushman." *Pictures Magazine* (June 3, 1916).

Henderson, L. R. S. "Chats with Players." *Motion Picture Magazine* (February 1915).

Hill, Wycliffe. "Most Handsome Man in Movies." *The Movie Magazine* (August 1915).

McGuirk, Charles J. "I Knew Them When." *Photoplay* (March 1925).

Smith, Frederick James. "Unwept, Unhonored and Unfilmed." *Photoplay* (July 1924).

John Bunny.

Francis X. Bushman and Ramon Novarro in *Ben-Hur* (1925).

Synon, Katherine. "Francis X. Bushman, Romanticist." *Photoplay* (July 1914).

Anonymous. "Bushman Wins the Big Contest." *Moving Picture World* (May 23, 1914).

Lon Chaney

Anderson, Robert G. *Faces, Forms and Films.* South Brunswick and New York: A. S. Barnes, and Company, 1971.

Bodeen, DeWitt. "Lon Chaney." *Focus on Film* (May-August 1970).

Chaney, Lon. "Motion Pictures." in *Encyclopedia Britannica*, editions of 1929-1933.

Howe, Herbert. "A Miracle Man of Make-Up." *Picture Play* (March 1920).

Kuttner, Alfred B. "Lon Chaney." *National Board of Review Magazine* (September 1930).

Mitchell, George. "Lon Chaney." *Films in Review* (December 1953).

Nyvett, Eleanor B. "Lon Chaney." *Bianco E. Nero* (July 1955).

Tully, Jim. "Lon Chaney." *Vanity Fair* (February 1928).

Ussher, Kathleen. "Chaney the Chameleon." *Pictures and Picturegoer* (March 1926).

———. "The Master of Menace." *Pictures and Picturegoer* (December 1927).

Anonymous. "A Master of Make-Up." *Pictures and Picturegoer* (March 1921).

———. "A Man of Many Faces." *Pictures and Picturegoer* (August 1922).

Charles Chaplin

Aguilas, Santiago. *El Genio Del Septimo Arte.* Madrid:

Norma Shearer and Lon Chaney in *He Who Gets Slapped* (1924).

Compania Iber Americana de Publicasiones, 1930.

Amengual, Barthelmy. *Charles Chaplin*. Algiers: Service de l'education, 1950.

Ausleger, Gerhard. *Charlie Chaplin*. Hamburg: Pfadweiser Verlag, 1924.

Baker, Peter. "Clown with a Frown." *Films and Filming* (August 1957).

Bakshy, Alexander. "A Knight Errant." *Dial* (May 1928).

Baldwin, Faith. "The Kingdom of Chaplin." *Modern Screen* (May 1931).

Bazin, André. "Si Charlot Ne Meure." *Cahiers Du Cinema* (November 1952).

Bessy, Maurice and Florey, Robert. *Monsieur Charlot ou La Rire Dans Le Nuit*. Paris: Jacques Damase, 1951.

Biby, Edward Alan. "How Pictures Found Charlie Chaplin." *Photoplay* (April 1919).

Bowman, W. Dodgson. *Charlie Chaplin*. New York: John Day, 1931.

Bravermann, Barnet G. "Charlie; a Close-Up of the Greatest of Comedians as Director." *Theatre Guild Magazine* (September 1930).

Brownlow, Kevin. "The Early Years of Charlie Chaplin." *Film* (No. 40).

———. "Watching Chaplin Direct *The Countess From Hong Kong*."*Film Culture* (Spring 1966).

Burger, Erich. *Charlie Chaplin*. Berlin: Rudolf Mosse Buchverlag, 1929.

Carr, Harry C. "Charlie Chaplin's Own Story." *Photoplay* (July—October 1915).

———. "A dozen Chaplins, and They're All Charlie."*Motion Picture Classic* (April 1919).

———. "Speech of Gold." *Motion Picture Magazine* (May 1922).

Chaplin, Charles. "What People Laugh At." *American Magazine* (November 1918).

———. *My Wonderful Visit*. London: Hurst and Blackett, 1922.

———. "Charlie Abroad." *Photoplay* (December

Merna Kennedy and Charles Chaplin in *The Circus*
(1928).

1921—January, 1922).

———. "My Trip Abroad." *Screenland* (June 1922).

———. "Does the Public Know What It Wants." *Adelphi* (January 1924).

———. "A Comedian Sees the World." *Woman's Home Companion* (September 1933-January 1934).

———. "The Future of the Silent Picture." *Windsor Magazine* (September 1936).

———. *My Autobiography*. London: The Bodley Head, 1964.

Chaplin, Charles Jr. *My Father, Charlie Chaplin*. New York: Random House, 1960.

Churchill, Winston. "Everybody's Language." *Collier's* (October 26, 1935).

Codd, Elsie. "Some First Impressions of Charlie Chaplin." *Pictures and Picturegoer* (October 11, 1919).

———. "Charles Chaplin, N. L. G." *Pictures and Picturegoer* (March 1927).

Collier, Lionel. "The Little Fellow." *Pictures and Picturegoer* (August 22, 1942).

Cook, William Wallace. "Pickles and Pearls." *Picture Play* (December 1915–April 1916).

Cook, Alistair. "Charlie Chaplin at Fifty" *The Atlantic Monthly* (August 1939).

Cotes, Peter and Thelma Niklaus. *The Little Fellow*. London: Paul Elek, 1951.

Crocker, Harry. "A Tribute to Charlie." *Academy Leader* (April 1972).

Curtis, Arthur E. "Just What Kind of a Fellow Is Charlie?" *Motography* (July 22, 1916).

D'Arne, Wilson. "One Man Movie Factory." *Pictures and Picturegoer* (November 23, 1935).

Darnton, Charles. "The Woman Who Found Charlie Chaplin." *Photoplay* (August 1934).

Delluc, Louis. *Charlie Chaplin*. London: John Lane Company, 1922.

Dyer, Peter John. "The True Face of Man." *Films and Filming* (September 1958).

Eisenstein, Sergei. "Charlie the Kid." *Sight and Sound* (Spring-Summer 1946).

Eubank, Victor. "The Funniest Man on the Screen." *Motion Picture Magazine* (March 1915).

Evans, Peter. "They Said It Was Impossible—But I Managed To See Chaplin." *Pictures and Picturegoer* (June 9, 1956).

Eyck, John Ten. "When Charlie Chaplin Earned $25 a Week." *Photoplay* (June 1917).

Farmer, Harcourt. "Is the Charlie Chaplin Vogue Passing?" *Theatre* (October 1919).

Fiske, Minnie Maddern. "The Art of Charles Chaplin." *Harper's Weekly* (May 6, 1916).

Florey, Robert. *Charles Chaplin*. Paris: Jean Pascal, 1927.

Fox, Fred W. "What Do You Really Know about Charlie Chaplin." *Motion Picture Director* (March 1926).

Franca, José-Augusto. *Charles Chaplin*. Lisbon: Inquerito, 1954.

Frank, Waldo David. "Charles Chaplin; a Portrait." *Scribner's* (September 1929).

Gaddis, Ivan. "Secret Griefs and Cankers in the Bosom." *Motion Picture Magazine* (April 1916).

Grau, Robert. "Why Charles Chaplin Declined." *Motion Picture Magazine* (October 1915).

Hayden, Kathlyn. "Charlie Gets the Bird." *Pictures and Picturegoer* (April 1931).

Hickey, Terry. "Accusations against Charles Chaplin for Political and Moral Offences." *Film Comment* (Winter 1969).

Hinxman, Margaret. "An Interview with Chaplin." *Sight and Sound* (Autumn 1957).

Hirsch, J. R. "The New Charlie Chaplin." *Motion Picture Magazine* (January 1916).

Holt, Paul. "The Loneliness of Chaplin." *Pictures and Picturegoer* (October 20, 1951).

Huff, Theodore. *Charlie Chaplin*. New York: Henry Schuman, 1951.

Jordan, Joan. "Mother o' Mine." *Photoplay* (July 1921).

Kenrick, J. N. "A Jinx on Chaplin's Leading Ladies." *Pictures and Picturegoer* (September 12, 1931).

Kisch, Egon Erwin. "I Work with Charlie Chaplin." *Living Age* (October 15, 1929).

Lang, Harry. "No Talkies for Charlie." *Photoplay* (May 1930).

Leprohon, Pierre. *Charles Chaplin*. Paris: André Bonne, 1970.

Lewin, Albert. "Dynamic Motion Pictures." *Shadowland* (October 1923).

Lyons, Timothy J. "Roland H. Totheroh Interviewed." *Film Culture* (Spring 1972).

McCaffrey, Donald W. *Four Great Comedians*. London: A. Zwemmer/South Brunswick and New York: A. S. Barnes and Company, 1968.

McDonald, Gerald. *The Picture History of Charlie Chaplin*. New York: Nostalgia Press, 1965.

———et al. *The Films of Charlie Chaplin*. New York: Citadel Press, 1965.

McGuirk, Charles J. "Chaplinitis." *Photoplay* (July—August 1915).

Mellor, G. J. "The Making of Charlie Chaplin." *Cinema Studies* (June 1966).

Melvin, John. "Is He Worth It." *Motion Picture Magazine* (February 1917).

Minney, R. "The Chaplin Nobody Knows." *Pictures and Picturegoer* (October 4, 1952—October 18, 1952).

———. *Chaplin, The Immortal Clown*. London: George Newnes, 1954.

Mitry, Jean. *Charlot Et La "Fabulation" Chaplinesque*. Paris: Editions Universitaires, 1957.

O'Higgins, Harvey. "Chaplin." *New Republic* (February 3, 1917).

Olden, John. "Behind the Screen." *Motion Picture Classic* (December 1916).

Payne, Robert. *The Great Charlie*. New York: Hermitage House, 1952.

Peltret, Elizabeth. "Chaplin's New Contract." *Photoplay* (February 1919).

Poulaille, Henry. *Charles Chaplin*. Paris: Bernard Gasset, 1927.

Quigley, Isabel. *Charlie Chaplin: Early Comedies*. London: Studio Vista, 1968.

Ramond, Edouard. *La Passion De Charlie Chaplin*. Paris: Librairie Baudiniere, 1927.

Ramsaye, Terry. "Chaplin and How He Does It." *Photoplay* (September 1917).

Raye, Martha. "Charles Chaplin." *Pictures and Picturegoer* (October 25, 1947).

Raynor, Henry. *Charlie Chaplin Intimé*. Paris: Gallimard, 1935.

Renoir, Jean. "Charlie among the Immortals." *Screenwriter* (July 1947).

Robinson, David. "Chaplin Meets the Press." *Sight and Sound* (Winter 1965—1966).

Rogers St. Johns, Adela. "The Loves of Charlie Chaplin." *Photoplay* (February 1923).

———. "Can a Genius Be a Husband." *Photoplay* (January 1927).

Rose, D. "Silence Is Requested." *Photoplay* (January 1927).

Rosen, Philip G. "The Chaplin World-View." *Cinema Journal* (Fall 1969).

Sadoul, Georges. *Vie De Charlot*. Paris: Les Editions Francais Reunis, 1952.

St. Johns, Ivan. "Everything's Rosy at Chaplin's." *Photoplay* (February 1926).

Simpson, Grace. "Groucho Looks at Charlie Chaplin." *Motion Picture Magazine* (May 1936).

Smith, Edward H. "Charlie Chaplin's Million Dollar Walk." *McClure's* (July 1916).

Smith, Frederick James. "The Tragic Comedian." *Shadowland* (November 1921).

Soupault, Philippe. *Charlot*. Paris: Librairie Plon, 1931.

Spears, Jack. "Chaplin's Collaborators." *Films In Review* (January 1962).

Spensley, Dorothy. "Come On Home, Charlie!" *Motion Picture Magazine* (September 1931).

Stevenson, Robert. "The Silence of Mr. Chaplin." *Nation and Athenaeum* (July 19, 1930).

Swaffer, Hannen. "Charlie Chaplin's Offence." *Pictures and Picturegoer* (June 13, 1931).

Taviner, Reginald. "What Love Has Done for Chaplin." *Photoplay* (October 1935).

Tyler, Parker. *Chaplin: Last of the Clowns*. New York: Vanguard Press, 1947.

Various. "Hands Off Love." *Transition* (September 1927).

———. "Témoignages sur *Limelight*," *Cahiers Du Cinema* (December 1952).

von Ulm, Gerith. *Charlie Chaplin: King of Tragedy*. London: Caxton, 1940.

Waley, H. D. "Is This Charlie?" *Sight and Sound* (Spring 1938).

Weinberg, Herman G. "Prelude to a Criticism of the Movies." *Close Up* (March 1931).

Whitcomb, E. V. "Charlie Chaplin." *Photoplay* (February 1915).

Wolf, William. "Charlie Chaplin Today—Elder Statesman of the Arts." *Show* (June 1972).

Wood, Leslie. "Lone Worker Charlie." *Amateur Cine World* (December 1952).

Wright, Willard H. "Chaplin's Great Secret." *Photoplay* (February 1922).

York, Cal. "Charlie's Unromantic Wedding." *Photoplay* (February 1925).

———. "Girl Wanted." *Photoplay* (January 1929).

Anonymous. "Chaplin To Strive for Quality." *Moving Picture World* (July 21, 1917).

———. "Special Chaplin Issue." *Pictures and Picturegoer* (June 7, 1919).

———. "Chaplin's Loyalty." *Pictures and Picturegoer* (March 1928).

———. "Les Films de Charlie Chaplin." *Image Et Son* (March 1957).

Syd Chaplin

Haskins, Harrison. "Mirth versus Millions." *Motion Picture Classic* (September 1919).

Betty Balfour and Syd Chaplin in *A Little Bit of Fluff,* released in the States by M-G-M as *Skirts.*

Anonymous. "Syd Chaplin." *Moving Picture World* (November 7, 1914).

———. "Syd Says." *Photoplay* (July 1920).

Marguerite Clark

Andrews, Muriel. "A Flower Garden Girl." *Picture Play Magazine* (November 1919).

Bacon, George. "Little Miss Practicality." *Photoplay* (March 1916).

Bodeen, De Witt. "Marguerite Clark." *Films In Review* (December 1964). *See also* issues of January, February, and March 1965 and October 1966.

Cheatham, Maude. "When Marguerite Says Good-Bye." *Motion Picture Classic* (October 1919).

De Piquet, Alice. "When Marguerite Hit Town." *Motion Picture Magazine* (August 1919).

Hall, Alice. "Marguerite Make-Believe." *Pictures and Picturegoer* (April 1921).

Hall, Gladys. "Marguerite Clark, a Girl That Is Different." *Motion Picture Magazine* (July 1915).

May, Lillian. "Why Marguerite Is Going To Stay in

Marguerite Clark.

Pictures." *Motion Picture Magazine* (February 1917).

Smith, Frederick James. "The Lilliput Lady." *Motion Picture Classic* (July 1921).

————. "Unwept, Unhonored and Unfilmed." *Photoplay* (July 1924).

Washburn, Beatrice. "Marguerite Clark—Today." *Photoplay* (April 1925).

Anonymous. "The Peter Pan of the Movies." *Photoplay* (December 1916).

————. "Biscuits and Beatitude à la Marguerite." *Theatre Magazine* (June 1919).

Betty Compson

Bodeen, DeWitt. "Betty Compson." *Films In Review* (August—September 1966). *See also* issues of October and November 1966 and December 1968.

Compson, Betty. "When My Chance Came." *Pictures and Picturegoer* (April 1921).

————. "Emotion To Order." *Pantomime* (September 28, 1921).

————. "A Week with the Stars: Sunday." *Photoplay* (November 1921).

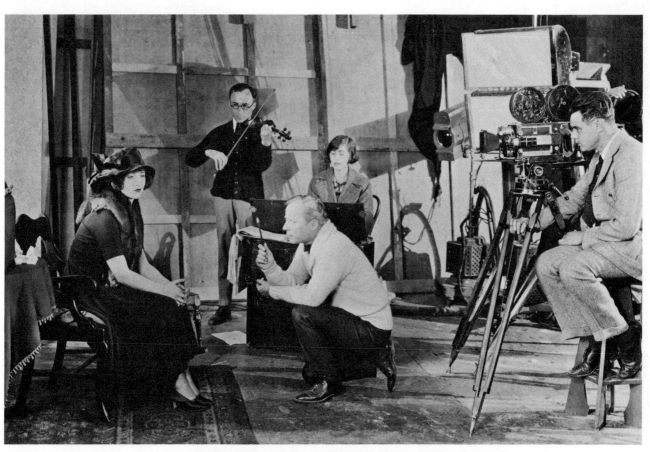

Herbert Brenon directs Betty Compson in *The Rustle of Silk* (1923).

Betty Compson.

———. "Richard Dix." *Photoplay* (June 1924).

———. "What Is Love?" *Photoplay* (June 1924).

———. "Acting in Talking Pictures." in *How Talkies Are Made*. Hollywood: Joe Bonica, 1930.

Dix, Richard. "Betty Compson." *Photoplay* (July 1924).

Fletcher, Adele Whitely. "Beauty—Brains—or Luck?" *Photoplay* (September 1930).

Foster, Dolores. "Too Many Guests." *Photoplay* (August 1930).

Goldbeck, Willis. "An Ideal in Star." *Motion Picture Magazine* (March 1922).

Howe, Herbert. "The Queen of Poverty Row." *Photoplay* (April 1929).

Mallinson, Russell. "The Sea of Success." *Pictures and Picturegoer* (July 1923).

Montanye, Lillian. "Strictly Business." *Motion Picture Classic* (June 1921).

Naylor, Hazel Simpson. "The Miracle Girl." *Motion Picture Magazine* (March 1921).

Peltret, Elizabeth. "Betty Compson—Romance Girl." *Motion Picture Classic* (December 1919).

Rogers St. Johns, Adela. "Betty and Jobyna." *Photoplay* (November 1923).

Smith, Frederick James. "B. C. 1920." *Motion Picture Classic* (June 1920).

Weber-Gould, Ruth. "A Yuletide Tale." *Picture Play* (January 1920).

Yost, Robert M. Jr. "Rescued from the River." *Photoplay* (December 1919).

Anonymous. "Betty Compson: The Girl on the Cover." *Pictures and Picturegoer* (November 1929).

Miriam Cooper

Blythe, Tony. "That Walsh Family." *Motion Picture Magazine* (November 1921).

Cheatham, Maude. "Fifty-Fifty." *Motion Picture Magazine* (August 1921).

Fletcher, Adele Whitely. "Miriam the Constant." *Motion Picture Magazine* (March 1920).

Howe, Herbert. "Hollywood Girls." *Motion Picture Magazine* (June 1922).

O'Dell, Paul. "Miriam Cooper: Forgotten Star." *The Silent Picture* (Autumn 1969). *See also* issues of Winter 1969/1970 and Spring and Summer 1970.

Old Timer, An. "Before They Were Stars: Miriam Cooper." *New York Dramatic Mirror* (May 15, 1920).

Anonymous. "Miriam Cooper Returns to the Screen." *Moving Picture World* (March 2, 1918).

———. "Dual Lives." *Photoplay* (September 1920).

———. "A Dark Star." *Pictures and Picturegoer* (April 1924).

Dolores Costello

Freund, Elizabeth. "Dolores Costello—Gallant Lady." *Photoplay* (February 1936).

Harrison, Paula. "A Favorite of Yours Returns." *Motion Picture Magazine* (April 1936).

St. Johns, Ivan. "The Exquisite Dolores." *Photoplay* (April 1926).

Anonymous. "Daughter of the Theatre." *Pictures and Picturegoer* (June 1930).

Joan Crawford

Biery, Ruth. "The Story of a Dancing Girl." *Photoplay* (September—November 1928).

Bourget, Jean-Loup. "Joan Crawford." *Positif* (October 1971).

Crawford, Joan. "The Job of Keeping at the Top." *Saturday Evening Post* (June 17, 1933).

———. *My Way of Life*. New York: Simon and Schuster, 1971.

———. and Jane Ardmore. *A Portrait of Joan*. New York: Doubleday, 1962.

Hughes, Frances. "Filmland's Royal Family, Second Edition." *Photoplay* (November 1929).

Quirk, Lawrence J. "Joan Crawford." *Films In Review* (December 1965). *See also* issues of June—July, 1966 and August—September 1966.

R.C. B. "Joan Was a Dancing Daughter, But Now—."*Pictures and Picturegoer* (January 23, 1932).

Rogers St. Johns, Adela. "Adela Rogers St. Johns Presents Joan Crawford Starring in the Dramatic Rise of a Self-Made Star." *Photoplay* (October-December 1937).

St. Johns, Ivan. "She Doesn't Use Lipstick in Public." *Photoplay* (May 1927).

Anonymous. "The Girl on the Cover." *Pictures and Picturegoer* (March 1929).

Bebe Daniels

Baxter, Jane McNaughton. "Whistler from Pig's Tails." *Picture Play* (November 1919).

Bodeen, De Witt. "Bebe Daniels." *Films In Review* (August—September 1964). *See also* issues of October, November, and December 1964.

Cheatham, Maude S. "Bebe, the Oriental." *Motion Picture Magazine* (November 1919).

Daniels, Bebe. "One Lesson the War Has Taught." *Photoplay World* (June 1919).

———. "56½ Miles per Hour." *Photoplay* (July 1921).

Miriam Cooper.

Dolores Costello as Mary in *Noah's Ark* (1928).

Joan Crawford and Harry Langdon in *Tramp, Tramp, Tramp* (1926).

———. "A Week with the Stars: Friday." *Photoplay* (November 1921).

———. "Why I Have Never Married." *Photoplay* (January 1924).

Daniels, Bebe, and Lyon, Ben. *Life with the Lyons.* London: Odhams Press, 1953.

Darnell, Jean. "Children of the Photoplay." *Photoplay* (December 1913).

Fletcher, Adele Whitely. "Beauty—Brains—or Luck?" *Photoplay* (October 1930).

Goldbeck, Willis. "In Black and Scarlet." *Motion Picture Classic* (September 1921).

Gordon, Ralph. "On Pomander Walk." *Motion Picture Magazine* (September 1920).

Henifin, Helen Starr. "The Luck of the Spanish." *Picture Play* (October, 1929). ·

Holt, Jack. "Bebe Daniels." *Photoplay* (July 1924).

Hyland, Dick. "Pictures or Football." *Photoplay* (September 1928).

Jordan, Joan. "A Belle of Bogota." *Photoplay* (January 1921).

Kingsley, Grace. "Her First Love Affair." *Picture Play* (September 1920).

Klumph, Helen. "Fun along the Way." *Picture Play* (January 1925).

Lang, Harry. "Bebe and Ben." *Photoplay* (July 1930).

Naylor, Hazel Simpson. "Sunlight on Black Laquer." *Motion Picture Magazine* (November 1921).

Remont, Fritzi. "A Daniels Come to Judgment." *Motion Picture Classic* (May 1919).

Rogers St. Johns, Adela. "The Most Popular Girl in Hollywood." *Photoplay* (November 1922).

Slide, Anthony. "Conversation with Bebe Daniels and Ben Lyon." *The Silent Picture* (Spring 1971).

Spensley, Dorothy. "The Evolution of Bebe." *Photoplay* (November 1925).

Various. "Bebe." *The Silent Picture* (Summer-Autumn 1971).

Marion Davies

Anderson, Earl. "Marion Davies." *Films In Review* (June-July 1972).

Broderick, Helen. "Pretty Soft To Be a Star, Eh?" *Photoplay* (September 1921).

Burke, Randolph Carroll. "Meet Marion Davies." *Pictures And Picturegoer* (July 4, 1931).

Collier, Lionel. "Shy and Subtle." *Pictures and Picturegoer* (April 1929).

Davies, Marion. "How I Keep in Condition." *Photoplay* (January 1922).

Marion Davies, with Louis B. Mayer, Norma Shearer, and Irving Thalberg.

Marion Davies.

Dillon, Franc. "Marion Davies — Angel of Mercy." *Pictures and Picturegoer* (September 21, 1935).

E. E. B. "Madcap Marion." *Pictures and Picturegoer* (August 1926).

Evans, Delight. "Galatea on Riverside Drive." *Photoplay* (October 1919).

Fletcher, Adele Whitely. "Rose and Old Lace." *Motion Picture Magazine* (September 1920).

Gaines, William P. "Davies' Secret of Success." *Photoplay* (February 1935).

Howe, Herbert. "The Local Favorite." *Photoplay* (May 1926).

Kendall, Philip. "Marion Davies." *The Silent Picture* (Summer 1970).

Lewis, Warren Woodruff. "Introducing Marion Davies." *Photoplay World* (June 1919).

McNamara, Sue. "Portraying a Princess." *Filmplay* (July 1922).

Milne, Tom. "Marion Davies." *Sight and Sound* (Autumn 1968).

Montanye, Lillian. "Marion of the Golden Hair." *Motion Picture Classic* (September 1919).

Old Timer, An. "Before They Were Stars: Marion Davies." *New York Dramatic Mirror* (May 8, 1920).

Rogers St. Johns, Adela. "An Impression of Marion Davies." *Photoplay* (January 1925).

Sheridan, Violet. "They Say It Never Happens—But It Does." *Motion Picture Magazine* (August 1918).

Werner, W. R. "That Was New York: Yellow Movies." *The New Yorker* (September 14, 1940).

York, Cal. "The Girl on the Cover." *Photoplay* (September 1926).

Anonymous. "The Magazine Cover Girl." *Pictures and Picturegoer* (March 1922).

———. "Beauty's Worth." *Pictures and Picturegoer* (August 1923).

———. "The Woman Who Has Never Lost a Friend." *Pictures and Picturegoer* (October 22, 1932).

Carol Dempster

Biery, Ruth. "I Don't Care If I Never Make Another Picture." *Photoplay* (August 1928).

Dorr, John. "The Movies, Mr. Griffith and Carol Dempster." *Cinema* (Fall 1971).

Evans, Delight. "Griffith's Newest Heroine." *Photoplay* (February 1922).

Hall, Gladys. "One of Us." *Motion Picture Magazine* (July 1922).

Herzog, Dorothy. "The Mystery Girl of Pictures." *Photoplay* (July 1925).

Carol Dempster, as *That Royle Girl* (1925).

———. "A Victim of Prejudice." *Photoplay* (March 1926).

Robbins, E. M. "The Two Strange Women." *Photoplay* (August 1919).

Schonert, Vernon L. "Carol Dempster." *Film Fan Monthly* (November 1971).

Smith, Frederick James. "Carol and Her Car." *Motion Picture Classic* (October 1920).

Dorothy Devore

Cheatham, Maude. "A Toiling Lily." *Motion Picture Magazine* (March 1921).

Slide, Anthony. "Dorothy Devore Interview." *The Silent Picture* (Summer 1972).

Douglas Fairbanks

Arms, Lucille. "Twenty Years from Now." *Pictures and Picturegoer* (July 1926).

Bates, Billy. "The Pickford-Fairbanks Wooing." *Photoplay* (June 1920).

Bent, Martin J. "The House That Mary Built." *Picture Play* (June 1920).

Bodeen, DeWitt. "Douglas Fairbanks." *Focus on Film* (November-December 1970).

Dorothy Devore.

Dorothy Devore and Babe London, two of the Christie Comedy Company's most popular stars.

Douglas Fairbanks, Sr., in *The Knickerbocker Buck-aroo* (1919).

Cohn, Alfred A. "A Photo Interview with Douglas Fairbanks." *Photoplay* (October 1917).

Cooke, Alistair. *Douglas Fairbanks: The Making of a Screen Character.* New York: Museum of Modern Art, 1940.

Eisenschitz, Bernard. *Douglas Fairbanks.* Paris: Anthologie du Cinema, 1969.

Evans, Alice Belton. "He Knows What He Wants and He Does It." *National Board of Review Magazine* (January 1928).

Fairbanks, Douglas. *Laugh and Live.* New York: Britton Publishing Company, 1917.

———. "Combining Play with Work." *American Magazine* (July 1917).

———. "Making Life Worth While." New York: Britton Publishing Company, 1918.

———. "Daring To Be a Dare Devil." *Pantomime* (September 28, 1917).

———. *My Secret Success.* Los Angeles: Photoplay Research Society, 1922.

———. "Let Me Say This for the Films." *Ladies Home Journal* (September 1922).

———. *Youth Points the Way.* New York: D. Appleton and Company, 1924.

———. "Why Big Pictures." *Ladies' Home Journal* (March 1924).

———. "What Is Love?" *Photoplay* (February 1925).

———. "The Magic Carpet of My Life, as Told to Stuart Jackson." *Pictures and Picturegoer* (March 18, 1933-April 1, 1933).

Fuhr, Charles Jr. "Douglas Fairbanks Was a Black Baby!" *Pictures and Picturegoer* (August 30, 1919).

Hall, Gladys and Adele Whitely Fletcher. "As They Were." *Motion Picture Magazine* (November 1920).

Hall, Leonard. "How about Mary and Doug." *Photoplay* (August 1930).

Hancock, Ralph and Fairbanks, Letitia. *Douglas Fairbanks: The Fourth Musketeer.* New York: Henry Holt, 1953.

Hornblow, Arthur Jr. "Douglas Fairbanks, Dramatic Dynamo." *Motion Picture Classic* (March 1917).

Lambert, Gavin. "Fairbanks and Valentino: The Last Heroes." *Sequence* (Summer 1949).

Lederer, Josie M. "The Persistent Honeymooners." *Pictures and Picturegoer* (January 1922).

Leloir, Maurice. *Cino Mois À Hollywood Avec Douglas Fairbanks.* Paris: J. Peyronnet, 1929.

Lindsay, Vachel. "The Great Douglas Fairbanks." *Ladies' Home Journal* (August 1926).

Livingstone, Will. "Douglas Fairbanks." *Photoplay World* (July 1919).

Mercer, Janet. "The Fairbanks Social War Is On." *Photoplay* (August 1936).

Minchinton, John. "Homespun Superman." *Films and Filming* (December 1954).

Naylor, Hazel Simpson. "The Fairbanks Scale of Americanism." *Motion Picture Magazine* (February 1919).

Owen, K. "Old Doc Cheerful." *Photoplay* (July 1916).

Pendleton, William. "What Future Ties for Doug Fairbanks." *Shadowplay* (April 1934).

R. H. "Interview with Douglas Fairbanks." *Close Up* (June 1930).

Rogers St. Johns, Adela. "Adela Rogers St. Johns' Story of the Married Life of Doug and Mary." *Photoplay* (February 1927).

Scognamillo, Giovanni. "Il Grande Doug o Quintesseza del l'Americanismo." *Bianco E. Nero* (June 1954).

Seitz, Carl W. "Douglas E. (Electricity) Fairbanks." *Motion Picture Magazine* (December 1916).

Smith, Frederick James. "Roping Doug Fairbanks into an Interview." *Motion Picture Classic* (September 1917).

Talmey, Allene. *Doug and Mary and Others.* New York: Macey-Masius, 1927.

Taylor, Charles H. "The Most Popular Man in the World." *Outlook* (December 24, 1924).

Thompson, E. R. "The Art of Douglas Fairbanks." *Pictures and Picturegoer* (June 1923).

Ussher, Kathleen. "Dynamo Doug." *Pictures and Picturegoer* (August 1925).

Anonymous. "Fairbanks Was an Old Man in '98." *Photoplay* (May 1917).
———. "Douglas Fairbanks Number." *Pictures and Picturegoer* (June 21, 1919).
———. "Desperado Doug" *Pictures and Picturegoer* (April 1926).
———. "The Future of Mary and Doug." *Pictures and Picturegoer* (May 7, 1932).
———. "Modest 'Doug Crusoe.' " *Pictures and Picturegoer* (December 31, 1932).

Charles Farrell

Bascom, Kirke. "Together Again." *Shadowplay* (February 1934).
Baskette, Kirtley. "The New Charles Farrell." *Photoplay* (December 1933).
Deaner, Frances. "Charlie's Impression of the Right Kind and the Wrong Kind of Girl." *Screen Mirror* (January 1931).
Manners, Dorothy. "All Is Fine and Dandy with the Charlie Farrells." *Motion Picture Magazine* (September 1931).
McKegg, William H. "Carefree Charlie." *Picture Play* (March 1929).
Simpson, Grace. "Charles the Unspoiled." *Pictures and Picturegoer* (December 1928).
Young, Cal. "Papa Stops Wondering." *Photoplay* (June 1927).

Charles Farrell and George Bancroft in *Old Ironsides* (1926).

Pauline Frederick

Barrett, E. E. "Little and Great." *Pictures and Picturegoer* (May 1927).
Bodeen, DeWitt. "Pauline Frederick." *Films In Review* (February 1965). *See also* issue of March 1965.
Bryers, Leslie. "Charms—and the Woman." *Motion Picture Magazine* (February 1922).
Frederick, Pauline. "The Story of My Life." *Motion Picture Magazine* (December 1918).
———. "Directors I Have Known." *Photoplay* (May 1919).
Gassaway, Gordon. "Polly Reforming Herself." *Pictures and Picturegoer* (February 1922).
Gregory, Nina Dorothy. "The 'Designing' Pauline Frederick." *Motion Picture Classic* (November 1917).
Johnson, Julian. "'Polly' Frederick." *Photoplay* (October 1915).
Lee, Carol. "Polly's Day at Home." *Motion Picture Classic* (January 1917).
Patterson, Ada. "The Tragedies of Pauline Frederick." *Photoplay* (April 1923).
Rogers St. Johns, Adela. "Kind to Dumb Waiters." *Photoplay* (May 1920).
———. "What Happened to Pauline Frederick." *Photoplay* (September 1926).
Seitz, Carl W. "Pauline Frederick." *Motion Picture Classic* (September 1917).
Squier, Emma-Lindsay. "They Call Her Polly." *Pictures and Picturegoer* (March 1921).

Greta Garbo

Adrian. "Adrian Answers 20 Questions on Garbo." *Photoplay* (September 1935).
Albert, Katherine. "What Garbo Thinks of Hollywood." *Photoplay* (August 1930).
Babcock, Muriel. "Will Television Mean the End of Garbo?" *Motion Picture Magazine* (October 1931).
Bainbridge, John. *Garbo*. London: Frederick Muller, 1955.
Barker, Sydney. "Player of Legend." *Players Showcase* (Summer 1965).
Baskette, Kirtley. "Is It Garbo or Hepburn?" *Photoplay* (March 1934).

Charles Farrell.

Pauline Frederick.

Greta Garbo in *The Kiss* (1929).

———. "Guessing Time for Garbo." *Photoplay* (September 1934).

Biery, Ruth. "The Story of Greta Garbo." *Photoplay* (April–June 1928).

Billquist, Fritiof. *Greta Garbo, Vedette Solitaire*. Paris: Librairie Artheme Fayard, 1959.

———. Garbo. London: Arthur Barker, 1960.

Blei, Franz. *Die Gottliche Garbo*. Giessen: Kindt & Bucher Verlag, 1930.

Boothe, Clare. "The Great Garbo." *Vanity Fair* (February 1932).

Brooks, Louise. "Women in Films." *Sight and Sound* (Winter 1958-1959).

Burke, Randolph Carroll. "Greta Garbo Talks about Her Ideal Man." *Pictures and Picturegoer* (June 6, 1931).

———. "Greta Garbo Hits Back." *Pictures and Picturegoer* (May 30, 1931).

Burnup, Peter. "Garbo Vindicated." *Pictures and Picturegoer* (February 20, 1932).

Canfield, Alyce. "The Garbo Legend." *Screen Guide* (October 1949).

C. B. "That Languid Lure." *Pictures and Picturegoer* (March 1928).

Clairmont, Leonard. "Greta Garbo Wanted To Be a Tight Rope Walker." *Photoplay* (May 1934).

Conway, Michael and others. *The Films of Greta Garbo*. New York: Citadel Press, 1963.

Culff, Robert. "Greta Garbo's Hollywood Silents." *The Silent Picture* (Autumn 1972).

Darte, Fernando. *Greta Garbo*. Rio Maior: Sintese, 1965.

Durgnat, Raymond, and John Kobal. *Greta Garbo*. London: Studio Vista, 1965.

Felbin, Gertrude. "Garbo's Authentic Life Story." *Pictures and Picturegoer* (July 14-August 4, 1934).

Gainsborough, Sally. "What Goulding Thinks of Garbo." *Pictures and Picturegoer* (June 18, 1932).

Garbo, Greta. "What the Public Wants." *Saturday Review* (June 13, 1931).

Hall, Leonard. "Garbo—Maniac." *Photoplay* (January 1930).

Herring, Robert. "Two Films and One Star." *Close Up* (December 1932).

Huff, Theodore. "The Career of Greta Garbo." *Films In Review* (December 1951).

Jordan, Allan. "Is Garbo Going Home?" *Movie Mirror* (December 1931).

Kuhn, Richard. *Greta Garbo*. Dresden: Carl Reissner Verlag, 1935.

Laing, E. E. *Greta Garbo: The Story of A Specialist*. London: John Gifford, 1946.

Levy, Allan. "Garbo Walks!" *Show* (June 1963).

Logan, Clarence A. "The Moon Goddess." *Pictures and Picturegoer* (January 5, 1935).

Makin, William J. *Greta Garbo*. London: C. Arthur Pearson, 1935.

Marshall, Herbert. "What It's Like To Work with Garbo." *Photoplay* (November 1934).

Mason, Jim. "Garbo Talks At Last." *Photoplay* (July 1936).

Maxwell, Virginia. "The Amazing Story Behind Garbo's Choice of Gilbert." *Photoplay* (January 1934).

Montesanti, Fausto. *Greta Garbo*. Rome: Canesi, 1963.

Mooring, W. H. "Going.....One Pair of Brogues....Garbo's Size." *Pictures and Picturegoer* (March 4, 1944).

Nordberg, Carl Eric. "Greta Garbo's Secret." *Film Comment* (Summer 1970).

Palmborg, Rilla Page. "The Private Life of Greta Garbo." *Photoplay* (September–October 1930).

———. *The Private Life of Greta Garbo*. New York: Doubleday Doran, 1931/London: John Long, 1932.

Phillips, Malcolm. "Greta Garbo's Front-Page Past." *Pictures and Picturegoer* (July 24, 1937).

Rankin, Ruth. "They're All Queening It." *Photoplay* (December 1933).

Ross, Virginia Peterson. "America Pro Tem." *New Yorker* (March 7, 1931).

Schuyler, Dorothy. "Garbo Visits Liz." *Photoplay* (August 1958).

Sheppard, Dick. "Hollywood's Biggest Comeback." *Photoplay* (November 1957).

Shirley, Lois. "The Girl Who Played Greta Garbo." *Photoplay* (August 1929).

Simmons, Jim. "I Won't Marry Stokowski Says Garbo." *Photoplay* (January 1938).

Sundborg, Ake. "That Gustafsson Girl." *Photoplay* (April–May 1930).

Swaffer, Hannen. "Hannen Swaffer Indicts Garbo and Gable." *Pictures and Picturegoer* (February 13, 1932).

Sylvia, Madame. "Garbo's Glamor—Mystery or Misery." *Photoplay* (December 1936).

Tully, Jim. "Greta Garbo." *Vanity Fair* (June 1928).

———. "Why Greta Is Great." *Pictures and Picturegoer* (October 5, 1935).

Tynan, Kenneth. "Garbo." *Sight and Sound* (April–June 1954).

Ussher, Kathleen. "A Swedish Siren." *Pictures and Picturegoer* (May 1927).

Wallin, John (Editor). *Garbo En Stjarnas Vrag*. Stockholm: Saxon & Lindstroms, 1955.

Waterbury, Ruth. "The Girl Jack Gilbert Married." *Photoplay* (July 1929).

West, Myrtle. "The Stockholm Venus." *Photoplay* (May 1926).

Wheelwright, Ralph. "The New Garbo." *Pictures and*

Picturegoer (September 30, 1933).
Wild, Roland. *Greta Garbo*. London: Rich and Cowan, 1933.
Williams, Marjory. "She Wanted To Be Alone." *Pictures and Picturegoer* (February 17, 1945).
Wilson, Harry D. "Why Garbo Plays Dumb." *Motion Picture Magazine* (August 1931).
Young, Cal. "What's the Matter with Garbo?" *Photoplay* (April 1927).
———. "They Think Alike!" *Photoplay* (June 1930).
Zeitlin, Ida. "Garbo Is Still Queen." *Motion Picture Magazine* (August 1936).
Zierold, Norman. *Garbo*. London: W. H. Allen, 1970.
Anonymous. "The Persistent Lovers." *Pictures and Picturegoer* (March 1930).

Gene Gauntier

Condon, Mabel. "Hot Chocolates and Reminiscences at Nine in the Morning." *Photoplay* (January 1915).

Gene Gauntier.

Gauntier, Gene. "A Voice from the Desert." *Moving Picture World* (March 2, 1912).
———. "Picture Players at a TurkishWedding." *Moving Picture World* (July 20, 1912).
———. "Gauntier Players in Ireland." *Moving Picture World* (October 4, 1913).
Smith, Frederick James. "Unwept, Unhonored and Unfilmed." *Photoplay* (July 1924).
Anonymous. "Miss Gauntier Returns from Europe." *Moving Picture World* (September 12, 1914).

Janet Gaynor

Albert, Katherine. "Janet Is Back on the Job." *Photoplay* (November 1930).
Bailey, Kent. "A Star Is Born Again." *Photoplay* (July 1937).
Bascom, Kirke. "Together Again." *Shadowplay* (February 1934).
Biery, Ruth Lieber. "Janet's Jonsey." *Photoplay* (October 1927).
Burke, Randolph Carroll. "The Gentle Art of Janet Gaynor." *Pictures and Picturegoer* (August 8, 1931).
Carr, Chauncey. "Janet Gaynor." *Films In Review* (October 1959). *See also* issue of May 1965.
Collier, Marjorie. "A Winner of Hearts." *Pictures and Picturegoer* (August 1930).
D'Arne, Wilson. "Janet Gaynor's Life Story." *Pictures and Picturegoer* (April 6–April 20, 1935).
Gaynor, Janet. "My Life — So Far — Told to Dorothy Spensley." *Photoplay* (December 1928-January 1929).
———. "Dreams Come True." *Pictures and Picturegoer* (October 8, 1932).
Guest, Wyndham. "Janet Gaynor and the Wrong Men." *Pictures and Picturegoer* (June 10, 1932).
Hayes, Barbara. "How Tyrone Power Won the Lonely Heart of Janet Gaynor." *Photoplay* (January 1938).
Lane, Jerry. "Why Men Go Mad Over Janet." *Motion Picture Magazine* (September 1936).
Manners, Dorothy. "Let's Get It Straight about Janet Gaynor." *Motion Picture Magazine* (December 1931).
M.D.P. "A Star Is Re-born." *Pictures and Picturegoer* (June 5, 1937).
Millet, Jean. "The Girl Who Is Getting the Breaks." *Photoplay* (January 1927).
Parsons, Harriet. "Janet Goes to War!" *Photoplay* (August 1930).
Wallace, Leonard. "Janet Gaynor." *Pictures and Picturegoer* (November 11, 1950).
Anonymous. "How Janet Chose." *Talking Screen* (January 1930).

Janet Gaynor and Gladys Brockwell as not too friendly sisters in *Seventh Heaven* (1927).

Janet Gaynor as Angela in *Street Angel* (1928).

———. "A Real Life Cinderella." *Pictures and Picturegoer* (September 23, 1933).

John Gilbert

Albert, Katherine. "Is Jack Gilbert Through?" *Photoplay* (February 1930).

Calhoun, Dorothy. "Why the Gilbert-Claire Marriage Failed." *Motion Picture Magazine* (November 1931).

Chute, Margaret. "The Boy Nobody Wanted." *Pictures and Picturegoer* (December 1926).

Cruikshank, Herbert Knight. "The Idol of the Hour." *Cinema Art* (April 1926).

Davis, Henry R. Jr. "A John Gilbert Index." *Films In Review* (October 1962).

Gilbert, John. "What Is Love." *Photoplay* (February 1925).

———. "Jack Gilbert Writes His Own Story." *Photoplay* (June — September 1928).

Lightfoot, Malcolm. "Jack Gilbert's Latest Heartbreak." *Shadowplay* (March 1934).

Maxwell, Virginia. "The Amazing Story Behind Garbo's Choice of Gilbert." *Photoplay* (January 1934).

———. "I Had To Leave Jack Gilbert—Virginia Bruce." *Photoplay* (April 1934).

Parker, Eleanor. "At Home with Jack Gilbert." *Pictures and Picturegoer* (August 27, 1932).

Quirk, Lawrence J. "John Gilbert." *Films In Review* (March 1956).

Rogers St. Johns, Adela. "Why Jack Gilbert Married." *Photoplay* (August 1929).

———. "What Defeated Jack Gilbert?" *Photoplay* (June 1935).

———. "The Tragic Truth about John Gilbert's Death." *Photoplay* (March 1936).

Shalbert, Elza. "John Gilbert Speaks at Last!" *Pictures and Picturegoer* (December 31, 1932).

Smith, Agnes. "Up Speaks a Gallant Loser." *Photoplay* (February 1927).

Greta Garbo and John Gilbert in *Flesh and the Devil* (1927).

Phyllis Haver and John Gilbert in *The Snob* (1924).

Spensley, Dorothy. "The Rival Nordic Lovers." *Photoplay* (October 1925).

St. Johns, Ivan. "I Told You So!" *Photoplay* (March 1925).

Tully, Jim. "John Gilbert." *Vanity Fair* (May 1928).

Waterbury, Ruth. "The Girl Jack Gilbert Married." *Photoplay* (July 1929).

Anonymous. "Only Twenty-Seven." *Pictures and Picturegoer* (June 1924).

Lillian and Dorothy Gish.

Dorothy Gish

Barrett, E. E. "Sweet Gish of Old Drury." *Pictures and Picturegoer* (January 1926).

Beach, Barbara. "The Worms Will Get You." *Motion Picture Classic* (November 1919).

Bodeen, DeWitt. "Dorothy Gish." *Films In Review* (August—September 1968).

Borden, Elizabeth. "The Girl on the Cover." *Photoplay* (August 1925).

Carr, Harry. "Three Little Girls Who Came Back." *Motion Picture Magazine* (August 1923).

Cheatham, Maude S. "Gattling Gun Gish." *Motion Picture Magazine* (August 1919).

Evans, Delight. "Seriously Speaking." *Photoplay* (November 1920).

Fletcher, Adele Whitely. "Beauty, Brains or Luck." *Photoplay* (August 1930).

Gish, Dorothy. "Largely a Matter of Love." *Photoplay* (March 1922).

———. "Lillian Gish, the Most Thoughtful Girl I Know." *Filmplay Journal* (April 1922).

———. "And So I Am a Comedienne." *Ladies Home Journal* (July 1925).

Gish, Lillian. "My Sister and I." *Theatre Magazine* (November 1927).

Hall, Gladys. "Mrs. Dorothy Gish Rennie." *Motion Picture Magazine* (June 1921).

Hall, Gladys, and Fletcher, Adele Whitely. "We Interview the Two Orphans." *Motion Picture Magazine* (May 1922).

Keefe, W. E. "Dorothy Gish." *Motion Picture Magazine* (June 1915).

Kremlin, Karl. "The Little Disturber Recovers." *Photo-Play Journal* (March 1919).

Patterson, Ada. "The Gish Girls Talk About Each Other." *Photoplay* (June 1921).

Remont, Fritzi. "Dorothy's War Story." *Motion Picture Classic* (May 1918).

Robbins, E.M. "Before and After Taking." *Motion Picture Classic* (January 1919).

Rogers St. Johns, Adela. "Black Sheep Gish." *Photoplay* (January 1919).

Willis, Richard. "I Go A-Calling on the Gish Girls." *Photoplay* (December 1914).

Wilson, Beatrice. "A Broken Set of Gishes." *Motion Picture Magazine* (April 1929).

Wright, Edna. "Dot Gish, Studio Star and Home Tomboy." *Motion Picture Magazine* (June 1917).

Anonymous. "A Tale of Two Gishes." *Pictures and Picturegoer* (May 1922).

———. "Gwyn — By Gish." *Motion Picture Director* (October 1926).

Lillian Gish

Blue, Monte. "Lillian Gish." *Photoplay* (July 1924).

Bodeen, DeWitt. "Lillian Gish: The Movies, Mr. Griffith and Me." *The Silent Picture* (Autumn 1969).

Brooks, Louise. "Women in Films." *Sight and Sound* (Winter 1957-1958).

Carr, Harry. "The Girl Who Is Different." *Motion Picture Magazine* (December 1925).

E.F.B. "A Saint in Silhouette." *Pictures and Picturegoer* (July 1926).

Evans, Delight. "The Girl on the Cover." *Photoplay* (December 1921).

Fletcher, Adele Whitely. "Beauty, Brains or Luck?" *Photoplay* (August 1930).

Gebhart, Myrtle. "Memories of Lillian Gish." *Pictures and Picturegoer* (October 1922).

Gish, Lillian. "Dorothy Gish, the Frankest Girl I Know." *Filmplay Journal* (April 1922).

———. "Beginning Young." *Ladies Home Journal* (September 1925).

———. "My Sister and I." *Theatre Magazine* (November 1927).

Lillian Gish as *Romola* (1925).

———. "D. W. Griffith: A Great American." *Harper's Bazaar* (October 1940).

———. "Silence Was Our Virtue." *Films and Filming* (December 1957).

———. The Movies, Mr. Griffith and Me. New Jersey: Prentice-Hall, 1969.

———. "Lillian Gish....Director." *The Silent Picture* (Spring 1970).

Grey, Marion. "And Villains Still Pursue Her." *Pictures and Picturegoer* (September 1921).

Hall, Gladys. "Lillian Gish." *Filmplay* (July 1922).

Hall, Gladys and Fletcher, Adele Whitely. "We Interview the Two Orphans." *Motion Picture Magazine* (May 1922).

Hall, Leonard. "Lillian Fights Alone." *Photoplay* (April 1929).

Hergesheimer, Joseph. "Lillian Gish." *American Mercury* (April 1924).

Johnson, Julian. "The Real Lillian Gish vs. the Imaginary." *Photoplay* (August 1918).

Morley, Sheridan. "Lillian Gish: Life and Living." *Films and Filming* (January 1970).

Old Timer, An. "Before They Were Stars: Lillian Gish." *New York Dramatic Mirror* (April 3, 1920).

Paine, Albert Bigelow. Life and Lillian Gish. New York: Macmillan, 1932.

Patterson, Ada. "The Gish Girls Talk about Each Other." *Photoplay* (June 1921).

Quirk, James R. "The Enigma of the Screen." *Photoplay* (March 1926).

Rochester, Paul. "What Love Means to Me." *Pictures and Picturegoer* (October 1924).

Scheuer, Philip K. "Reminiscing with Lillian Gish." *Los Angeles Times* (December 22, 1968).

Smith, Frederick James. "The Lyric Lady." *Motion Picture Classic* (September 1919).

Stern, Harold. "The Age of Innocence Returns." *After Dark* (June 1969).

Tozzi, Romano. "Lillian Gish." *Films In Review* (December 1962). *See also* issue of April 1964.

Wagenknecht, Edward. Lillian Gish, An Interpretation. Washington: University of Washington Bookstore, 1927.

Williams, Louise. "My Friend Lillian Gish." *Picture Play* (November 1920).

Willis, Richard. "I Go A-Calling on the Gish Girls." *Photoplay* (December 1914).

Wilson, Beatrice. "A Broken Set of Gishes." *Motion Picture Magazine* (April 1929).

Anonymous. "Lillian Gish." *Moving Picture World* (June 20, 1914).

———. "A Tale of Two Gishes." *Pictures and Picturegoer* (May 1922).

———. "Conversation with Lillian Gish." *Sight and Sound* (Winter 1957-1958).

Louise Glaum.

Louise Glaum

Bruce, Betsy. "T'Was Ever Thus." *Motion Picture Magazine* (September 1920).

Dew, Robert. "Siren Stuff." *Motion Picture Magazine* (March 1922).

Howe, Herbert. "Living Down the Past." *Motion Picture Classic* (December 1917).

———. "Vampire or Ingenue." *Photoplay* (August 1918).

Lee, Carol. "A Vampire Who's Proud of It." *Motion Picture Classic* (March 1917).

Milton, Martha. "I've Vamped Enough." *Motion Picture Classic* (August 1918).

Ogden, Helen. "The Lure of Peacock Feathers." *Picture Play* (March 1920).

Smith, Frederick James. "Unwept, Unhonored and Unfilmed." *Photoplay* (July 1924).

Taylor, Mary Keane. "The Luxurious Louise." *Motion Picture Classic* (June 1919).

Jetta Goudal

Busby, Marquis. "Sunday Night at Jetta's." *Photoplay* (May 1930).

Clark, Francis. "Jetta Lives Down Her Past." *Photoplay* (August 1927).

Howe, Herbert. "A Parisien Chinese Lily." *Photoplay* (August 1923).

Ussher, Kathleen. "A Human Cocktail." *Pictures and Picturegoer* (November 1927).

Anonymous. "Three New Faces." *Photoplay* (July 1923).

Corinne Griffith

Bell, Caroline. "The Very Unexpected." *Picture Play* (June 1920).

Boone, Arabella. "Why Bob Your Hair?" *Photoplay* (July 1920).

Busby, Marquis. "Exit—Corinne Griffith." *Photoplay* (May 1930).

Craig, Marion. "Frapped in Flatbush." *Photoplay* (January 1919).

Evans, Delight. "The Girl on the Cover." *Photoplay* (January 1922).

Fletcher, Adele Whitely. "Instead of the Orchard." *Motion Picture Classic* (March 1921).

Griffith, Corinne. "How I Keep in Condition." *Photoplay* (November 1921).

———. "Frank Mayo and Conway Tearle." *Photoplay* (June 1924).

Corinne Griffith.

Corinne Griffith and Conway Tearle in *Black Oxen* (1924).

Robert Harron.

Rogers St. Johns, Adela. "Why Men Go Crazy about Corinne Griffith." *Photoplay* (December 1923).

Smith, Frederick James. "Corinne, Chocolate Cake and a Deep, Dark Secret." *Motion Picture Classic* (April 1919).

———. "Beauty and the Interviewer." *Motion Picture Magazine* (January 1922).

Tearle, Conway. "Corinne Griffith." *Photoplay* (July 1924).

Anonymous. "A Man's Woman." *Pictures and Picturegoer* (July 1924).

Robert Harron

Dunham, Harold. "Bobby Harron." *Films In Review* (December 1963). *See also* issues of April and October 1968.

———. "Mae Marsh, Robert Harron and D. W. Griffith." *The Silent Picture* (Autumn 1969).

Hall, Gladys. "Unchanging." *Motion Picture Magazine* (December 1920).

Handy, Truman B. "Buoyant Bobby." *Motion Picture Magazine* (September 1919).

North, Jean. "Digging Up the Acorn." *Photoplay* (October 1920).

Peltret, Elizabeth. "Griffith's Boy—Bobby." *Motion Picture Magazine* (September 1919).

Smith, Frederick James. "Bashful Bobbie." *Motion Picture Classic* (July 1920).

Willis, Richard. "Three Rough Necks from *The Escape*." *Photoplay* (February 1915).

William S. Hart as Patrick Henry in his 1903 stage success, *Hearts Courageous.*

William S. Hart

Blaisdell, George. "Bill Hart Hits the Great White Trail." *Moving Picture World* (June 2, 1917).

Cheatham, Maude. "Bill Hart's Dream House." *Motion Picture Classic* (August 1920).

———. "Desert Heart." *Motion Picture Magazine* (April 1921).

———. "And They Live Happily." *Motion Picture Magazine* (June 1922).

Codd, Elsie. "The Retirement of Bill Hart." *Pictures and Picturegoer* (April 1921).

———. "Good Man—Bad Man." *Pictures and Picturegoer* (February 1922).

Conlon, Paul Hubert. "Out in the Open with Bill." *Picture Play* (September 1920).

Daugherty, Frank. "Ol' Bill Hart Is Coming Back!" *Photoplay* (December 1930).

De Salto, George. "Hart of the Plains." *Photoplay* (October 1915).

Duffy, Gerald C. "Cupid Thought He Could Out-Shoot Hart." *Motion Picture Classic* (October 1918).

Flagg, James Montgomery. "Out from the West." *Photoplay* (May 1922).

Fletcher, Adele Whitely. "Bill Hart." *Motion Picture Magazine* (February 1922).

Fuir, Charles. "The Most Popular Horse in Films." *Motion Picture Magazine* (January 1918).

Gainn, Arthur Jr. "Bad Man Kill Bad Man." *Picture Play* (September 1916).

Gordon, Gertrude. "William S. Hart, the Man of the West." *Motion Picture Magazine* (November 1916).

Hart, William S. "Living Your Characters." *Motion Picture Magazine* (May 1917).

———. "How I Got In." *Motion Picture Magazine* (December 1917).

———. "Cowpunchers of the Antipodes." *Photoplay* (April 1919).

———. "And They Are All Beautiful." *Motion Picture Magazine* (August 1919).

William S. Hart and Clara Williams in *Hell's Hinges* (1916).

————. "My Pinto and Me." *Photoplay* (February 1920).

————. "The Compleat Cowboy." *Pictures and Picturegoer* (September 1921).

————. *Told Under A White Oak*. Boston: Houghton Mifflin, 1922.

————. *My Life East and West*. Boston: Houghton Mifflin, 1929.

Longford, Marion Howe. "An' Oh, the Heart of Him." *Motion Picture Classic* (August 1918).

Mistley, Media. "Presenting Your Bill." *Photo-Play Journal* (February 1919).

Mitchell, George J. "William S. Hart." *Films In Review* (April 1955).

————. "The William S. Hart Museum." *Films In Review* (August-September 1962).

Moore, William. "On Tour with Bill Hart." *Motion Picture Magazine* (January 1918).

Naylor, Hazel Simpson. "On Tour with Bill Hart." *Motion Picture Classic* (November 1917).

————. "The Hungry Hart." *Motion Picture Magazine* (March 1919).

Patterson, Ada. "Bill Hart's True Love." *Photoplay* (January 1921).

Rogers St. Johns, Adela. "Bill Hart's Bride Has Him Thrown, Tied, Branded and Feeds His Bulldog Caramels." *Photoplay* (April 1922).

Shaffer, Rosalind. "After Four Years." *Photoplay* (October 1929).

Shirk, Adam Hull. "Bill Hart Reminisces." *Motion Picture Director* (January 1926).

Vosges, Hilary. "What Bill Hart Told in the Maid's

Room.'' *Photoplay* (September 1917).
Anonymous. ''The Stage Career of William S. Hart: 1898–1912.'' *The Silent Picture* (Autumn 1972).

Emil Jannings

Collier, Lionel. ''Something in the Herr.'' *Pictures and Picturegoer* (January 1929).
———. ''Re-enter Jannings.'' *Pictures and Picturegoer* (September 1930).
Dreyer, Carl. ''Sur un Film de Jannings,'' and ''Du Jeu de l'acteur.'' *Cahiers Du Cinema* (January 1962).
Ford, Charles. *Emil Jannings*. Paris: Anthologie du Cinéma, 1969.
Howe, Herbert. ''Four Kings from Brooklyn.'' *Photoplay* (January 1923).
Ihering, Herbert. *Emil Jannings*. Berlin: Verlagsastalt Huthig, 1941.
Jannings, Emil and Bergius, C. C. *Theater, Film – Das Leben Und Ich*. Berchtesgaden: Verlag Zimmer & Herzog, 1961.
Johnson, Julian. A Visit with Emil Jannings.'' *Photoplay* (February 1926).
Scognamillo, Giovanni. ''Emil Jannings, Mostro Sacro

Emil Jannings as General Dolgorucki in *The Last Command* (1928).

de Cinema Tedasco.'' *Bianco E Nero* (October 1953).
Smith, Frederick James. ''The Big Boy from Berlin Is Here.'' *Photoplay* (December 1926).
Strider, Gary. ''Emil Jannings.'' *Screenland* (January 1927).
Truscott, Harold. ''Emil Jannings, a Personal View.'' *The Silent Picture* (Autumn 1970).
Tully, Jim. ''Emil Jannings.'' *Vanity Fair* (November 1927).
Anonymous. ''Jannings from Germany.'' *Pictures and Picturegoer* (May 1924).

Buck Jones

E. E. B. ''Buck Goes Abroad.'' *Pictures and Picturegoer* (May 1926).
Jones, Buck. ''Horses.'' *Pictures and Picturegoer* (August 1921).
Jordan, Joan. ''A Rodeo Romeo.'' *Photoplay* (October 1921).

Emil Jannings.

Charles "Buck" Jones and Jane Novak in *Lazybones* (1925).

Tully, Jim. "A Top Rider." *Photoplay* (January 1926).

Anonymous. "The Eternal Cowboy." *Pictures and Picturegoer* (March 1925).

Alice Joyce

Andrews, Muriel. "Her Infinite Variety." *Picture Play* (March 1920).

Barrett, E.E. "Alice in Londonland." *Pictures and Picturegoer* (April 1928).

Bruce, Betsy. "Alice a la Mode." *Motion Picture Magazine* (April–May 1920).

Durling, E. V. "Alice Where Have You Been?" *Photoplay* (May 1924).

Fletcher, Adele Whitely. "Beauty, Brains or Luck?" *Photoplay* (September 1930).

Gaddis, Pearl. "Alice Joyce—Honeymoon Truant." *Photoplay* (May 1915).

Hall, Gladys. "The Honeymoon and Sixpence." *Motion Picture Magazine* (July 1920).

Johnson, Julian. "Clan Moore." *Photoplay* (December 1918).

Martin, Minerva. "Alice Joyce Advises." *Photoplay* (July 1914).

Patterson, Ada. "Call for Alice Joyce." *Photoplay* (February 1920).

———. "The Lady of Vast Silences." *Photoplay* (March 1920).

Prescott, William. "Oh, Joyce! She's In Again." *Picture Play* (September 1916).

Smith, Frederick James. "Alice for Short." *Photoplay* (October 1917).

———. "Alice in Quest of a Temperament." *Motion*

Alice Joyce and Conway Tearle in *Dancing Mothers* (1926).

Picture Classic (December 1918).

Williams, Louise. "Alice Unreserved." *Picture Play* (July 1920).

York, Cal. "The Girl on the Cover." *Photoplay* (October 1926).

Buster Keaton

Benayonn, Robert. "Le Regard de Buster Keaton." *Positif* (Summer 1966).

Bishop, Christopher. "The Great Stone Face." *Film Quarterly* (Fall 1958).

Blesh, Rudi. *Keaton.* New York: MacMillan, 1966.

Breen, Max. "Behind the Dead Pan." *Pictures and Picturegoer* (March 21, 1936).

Brownlow, Kevin. "Buster Keaton." *Film* (No. 42).

Coursodon, Jean Pierre. *Keaton Et Cie.* Paris: Editions Seghers, 1964.

Denis, Michel. *Buster Keaton.* Paris: Anthologie de Cinéma, 1971.

Friedman, Arthur B. "Buster Keaton: An Interview." *Film Quarterly* (Summer 1966).

Gillet, John, and Blue, James. "Keaton at Venice." *Sight and Sound* (Winter 1965–1966).

Goldbeck, Willis. "Only Three Weeks." *Motion Picture Magazine* (October 1921).

Houston, Penelope. "The Great Blank Page." *Sight and Sound* (Spring 1968).

Keaton, Buster. "Why I Never Smile." *Ladies Home Journal* (June 1926).

———. "A Quatre Temps." *Cahiers Du Cinema* (April 1962).

Keaton, Buster and Samuels, Charles. *My Wonderful World of Slapstick.* New York: Doubleday, 1960.

Keaton, Joe. "The Cyclone Baby." *Photoplay* (May 1927).

Laura, Ernesto G. "Buster Keaton Nel Periodo Muto." *Bianco E Nero* (September–October 1963).

Buster Keaton as *The Navigator* (1924).

Buster Keaton in his last "great" screen appearance, *A Funny Thing Happened on the Way to the Forum* (1966).

Lebel, Jean-Patrick. *Buster Keaton*. London: A. Zwemmer, 1967.

McCaffrey, Donald W. *Four Great Comedians*. London: A. Zwemmer, 1968/South Brunswick and New York: A. S. Barnes and Company, 1968.

Mulligan, W. E. "The Man Who Never Smiles." *Pantomime* (October 5, 1921).

Oms, Marcel. *Buster Keaton*. Lyon: Serdoc, 1964.

Peltret, Elizabeth. "Poor Child!" *Motion Picture Classic* (March 1921).

P. R. M. "The Mournful Mirthmaker." *Pictures and Picturegoer* (October 1922).

Robinson, David. *Buster Keaton*. London: Secker and Warburg, 1969.

———. "Buster." *Sight and Sound* (Winter 1959-1960).

Rogers St. Johns, Adela. "Interviewing Joseph Talmadge Keaton." *Photoplay* (October 1922).

Russell, Spencer. "Hard Knocks Make a Man." *Filmplay* (July 1922).

Talmadge, Mr. Natalie. "Before and After Taking." *Photoplay* (September 1921).

Various. "Buster Keaton a n'en plus finir." *Cinema 66* (April 1966).

Anonymous. "His Frozen Face is Certainly His Fortune." *Pictures and Picturegoer* (October 3, 1931).

Annette Kellerman

Howe, Selma. "Annette Is Back Again." *Picture Play* (August 1920).

MacMahon, Henry. "Annette Kellerman." *Motion Picture Classic* (February 1917).

Peltret, Elizabeth. "The Pride of the Anzacs." *Motion Picture Classic* (June 1920).

Anonymous. "Stars and Sharks." *Pictures and Picturegoer* (August 26, 1916).

Annette Kellerman in *A Daughter of the Gods* (1916).

J. Warren Kerrigan

Baker, Hettie Gray. "What Warren Kerrigan Isn't." *Motion Picture Magazine* (May 1915).

Chapman, Jay Brien. "Leading a Double Life." *Motion Picture Magazine* (October 1919).

Henry, William M. "The Great God Kerrigan." *Photoplay* (February 1916).

Kerrigan, J. Warren. "My Most Exciting Experience Near the Touch of Death." *Photoplay* (June 1914).

Mayne, Marjorie. "Kerrigan Comes Back." *Pictures and Picturegoer* (April 1924).

Peterson, Elizabeth. "Kerrigan's Home Life Ideal." *Motion Picture Classic* (December 1916).

Remont, Fritzi. "Sonny." *Motion Picture Magazine* (May 1918).

Robinson, Carlyle R. "If Dreams Come True." *Motion Picture Classic* (October 1917).

"Autobiography of J. Warren Kerrigan." *Universal Weekly* (June 27, 1914).

Barbara La Marr

Bronnen, Arnolt. *Film Und Leben Barbara La Marr.* Linz: Ibis Verlag, 1947.

Barbara La Marr.

J. Warren Kerrigan.

Dougherty, Jack. "Why I Quit Being Mr. Barbara La Marr." *Photoplay* (October 1924).

Drummond, Joan. "Beautiful Barbara." *Pictures and Picturegoer* (April 1924).

Klumph, Helen. "When Is Barbara Sincere?" *Picture Play* (September 1923).

La Marr, Barbara. "Why I Adopted a Baby." *Photoplay* (May 1923).

———. "My Screen Lovers." *Photoplay* (November 1923).

———. "Lew Cody." *Photoplay* (June 1924).

Lyon, Ben. "Vampires I Have Known." *Photoplay* (February 1925).

Rogers St. Johns, Adela. "The Girl Who Was Too Beautiful." *Photoplay* (June 1922).

———. "Hail and Farewell." *Photoplay* (April 1926).

Uselton, Roi A. "Barbara La Marr." *Films In Review* (June–July, 1964).

Woodridge, A. L. "Phantom Daddies of the Screen." *Photoplay* (January 1934).

York, Cal. "Can Barbara Come Back?" *Photoplay* (January 1926).

Harry Langdon

Hall, Leonard. "Hey! Hey! Harry's Coming Back." *Photoplay* (June 1929).

Harry Langdon in *The Chaser* (1928).

McCaffrey, Donald W. *Four Great Comedians.* London: A. Zwemmer, 1969/South Brunswick and New York: A. S. Barnes and Company, 1969.

Monks, Margaret G. "Harry, Harry, Quite Contrary." *Cinema Art* (October 1926).

North, Jean. "It's No Joke To Be Funny." *Photoplay* (June 1925).

Schonert, Vernon L. "Harry Langdon." *Films In Review* (October 1967). *See also* issues of November and December 1967.

Vitoux, Frederic. "Harry Langdon et Frank Capra." *Positif* (December 1971).

Laura La Plante

Barrett, E. E. "Ain't She Sweet." *Pictures and Picturegoer* (July 1927).

Denny, Reginald. "Laura La Plante." *Photoplay* (July 1924).

La Plante, Laura. "A Letter from Location." *Picture Play* (May 1925).

Summers, Murray. "Laura La Plante in 'Her Reel Life.'" *Filmograph* (Volume II, Nos. 3 and 4).

Tully, Jim. "Laura La Plante." *Vanity Fair* (January 1928).

Joseph Schildkraut, Emily Fitzroy, and Laura La Plante in *Show Boat* (1929).

Jones, Gladys. "A Breakfast Chat with Florence Lawrence." *Feature Movie Magazine* (March 1916).

Katterjohn, Monte M. "Growing Up with the Movies." *Photoplay* (November 1914–February 1915).

Lawrence, Florence. "Just about Myself." *Pictures and Picturegoer* (April 18, 1914).

———. "Why I Came Back." *Motion Picture Magazine* (March 1916).

Rogers St. Johns, Adela. "The Return of Florence Lawrence." *Photoplay* (May 1921).

Smith, Frederick James. "Unwept, Unhonored and Unfilmed." *Photoplay* (July 1924).

Anonymous. "The Girl of a Thousand Faces." *New York Sunday Post-Dispatch Magazine* (March 20, 1910).

———. "Florence Lawrence Joins Independents." *Moving Picture World* (May 18, 1912).

———. "Florence Lawrence—Famous Picture Star." *New York Dramatic Mirror* (July 31, 1912).

Borde, Raymond. "L'Insolence de Harold Lloyd." *Positif* (Summer, 1966).

———. *Harold Lloyd.* Paris: Premier Plan, 1968.

Brundidge, Harry T. "Who'll Wear These Glasses." *Motion Picture Story Magazine* (November 1934).

Cahn, William. *Harold Lloyd's World of Comedy.* London: Allen and Unwin, 1966.

Chute, Margaret. "The Business Comedian." *Pictures and Picturegoer* (February 1927).

Fredericks, James. "Lloyd: Laughsmith." *Motion Picture Magazine* (April–May 1920).

Friedman, Arthur B. "Interview with Harold Lloyd." *Film Quarterly* (Summer 1962).

Furman, Bess. "Alias Desperate Jack Dalton." *Motion Picture Magazine* (August 1921).

Ganley, Harry. "Up through the Years with Harold Lloyd." *Motion Picture Magazine* (February 1936).

Garringer, Nelson E. "Harold Lloyd." *Films In Review* (August–September 1962).

Granger, Frank. "Five Hundred a Laugh." *Motion*

Florence Lawrence.

Harold Lloyd in *The Kid Brother* (1927).

Picture Magazine (June 1919).

Hall, Gladys and Adele Whitely Fletcher. "We Interview the Boy." *Motion Picture Magazine* (July 1922).

Howe, Herbert. "Out of His Shell." *Motion Picture Classic* (October 1922).

Kaminsky, Stuart. "Harold Lloyd, a Reassessment of His Film Comedy." *The Silent Picture* (Autumn 1972).

Kennedy, John B. "It Pays To Be Sappy." *Collier's* (June 11, 1927).

Lacourbe, Roland. *Harold Lloyd.* Paris: Editions Seghers, 1970.

Laurel, Marie. "Harold Lloyd, the Happy Comedian." *Motion Picture Classic* (October 1919).

Leigh, Anabel. "Specs without Glass." *Photoplay* (January 1920).

Lloyd, Harold. "For the People, by the People." *Filmplay Journal* (April 1922).

———. "The Autobiography of Harold Lloyd." *Photoplay* (May-July 1924).

———. "What Is Love." *Photoplay* (February 1925).

———. "When They Gave Me the Air." *Ladies Home Journal* (February 1928).

———. "Looking at the World through Horn-Rimmed Specs." *Motion Picture Magazine* (September 1933).

———. "Bombed into Fame." *Pictures and Picturegoer* (October 15, 1932).

———. "The Funny Side of Life." *Films and Filming* (January 1964).

———. "The Serious Business of Being Funny." *Film Comment* (Fall 1969).

Lloyd, Harold and Stout W. Wesley. *An American Comedy.* New York: Longmans Green, 1928.

McCaffrey, Donald W. *Four Great Comedians.* London: A. Zwemmer, 1968/South Brunswick and New York: A. S. Barnes and Company, 1968.

Mullett, Mary B. "A Movie Star Who Knows What Makes You Laugh." *American Magazine* (July 1922).

Proctor, Kay. "Up to His Old Tricks." *Movieland* (October 1964).

Reddy, Joseph. "Thrills and Chills in the Filming of Harold Lloyd's *Feet First.*" *Screen Mirror* (October 1930).

Reid, Margaret. "Looking on with an Extra Girl." *Picture Play* (June 1925).

Rogers St. Johns, Adela. "What about Harold Lloyd." *Photoplay* (August 1922).

———. "How Lloyd Made *Safety Last.*" *Photoplay* (July 1923).

Sherwood, Robert E. "The Perennial Freshman." *New Yorker* (January 30, 1926).

Taylor, Sam. "Directing Harold Lloyd." *Motion Picture Director* (November 1925).

Wallace, Leonard. "Harold Lloyd." *Pictures and Picturegoer* (November 1925).

Anonymous. "Harold Lloyd or 'Lonesome Luke.'" *Moving Picture World* (April 7, 1917).

———. "Harold Speaks Up." *Talking Screen* (January 1930).

Bessie Love

Barrett, E.E. "The Girl on the Cover." *Pictures and Picturegoer* (August 1929).

Breen, Max. "Love Comes In at the Door." *Pictures and Picturegoer* (August 1, 1936).

Carr, Harry. "Three Little Girls Who Came Back." *Motion Picture Magazine* (August 1923).

Clifford, Graham. "Bessie Love and the 'Cry Baby Face.'" *Photo-Play World* (June 1919).

Collier, Marjory. "The Bow Bells of Broadway." *Pictures and Picturegoer* (June 1930).

Curley, Kenneth. "The Idealist Speaks." *Motion Picture Magazine* (May 1922).

Dunham, Harold. "Bessie Love." *Films In Review* (February 1959). *See also* issue of June–July 1959.

Gassaway Gordon. "Bonnie Sweet Bessie." *Motion Picture Classic* (August 1922).

Bessie Love.

Bessie Love and Richard Barthelmess in *Soul-Fire* (1925).

Handy, Truman B. "Bessie Love Grows Up." *Pictures and Picturegoer* (July 1921).

Howe, Herbert. "The Girl Who Walked Back." *Photoplay* (May 1929).

Love, Bessie. "The Other Side of the Camera." *Films and Filming* (July 1962).

———. "Jokers Wild." *Films and Filming* (August 1966).

Montanye, Lillian. "When Bessie Love Was Lost in New York." *Motion Picture Magazine* (April 1918).

Peltret, Elizabeth. "Bessie Love." *Motion Picture Classic* (September 1920).

Ryan, Wallace. "Bessie Love and Hayakawa." *Photoplay* (September 1921).

Sayford, I. S. "Just a Little Love." *Photoplay* (August 1916).

St. Johns, Ivan. "The Little Brown Wren." *Photoplay* (January 1925).

Ten Eyck, John. "'Agate Bessie' the Marble Gambolier." *Photoplay* (August 1917).

Todd, Stanley. "The Rise of Bessie Love." *Motion Picture Magazine* (October 1917).

Anonymous. "Bessie Love, New Pathe Star." *Moving Picture World*. (November 3, 1917).

———. "Wrong about Face." *Photoplay* (December 1919).

———. "Bessie Love Checklist." *Monthly Film Bulletin* (February 1972).

Ben Lyon

Busby, Marquis. "A Great Come-Back." *Photoplay* (September 1930).

Daniels, Bebe and Lyon, Ben. *Life with the Lyons.* London: Odhams Press, 1953.

Lonergan, Elizabeth. "Ben Lyon." *Pictures and Picturegoer* (April 1925).

Lyon, Ben. "Vampires I Have Known." *Photoplay* (February 1925).

Pinker, John B. "Ben Lyon Is Always a Lamb." *Pictures and Picturegoer* (January 30, 1932).

Rogers St. Johns, Adela. "Hollywood's New Heart Breaker." *Photoplay* (January 1925).

Slide, Anthony. "Bebe Daniels and Ben Lyon in Conversation" and "The Films of Ben Lyon." *The Silent Picture* (Spring 1971).

Dorothy Mackaill

Burton, Stanley. "Second Thoughts on Matrimony." *Photoplay* (March 1930).

Collier, Marjory. "The Lass from Yorkshire." *Pictures and Picturegoer* (September 1930).

Gebhart, Myrtle. "She Knows What She Wants—and Will Get It." *Picture Play* (January 1925).

———. "Would You Marry an Actor?" *Picture Play* (May 1925).

Mackaill, Dorothy. "What Is Love" *Photoplay* (May 1925).

Percy Marmont and Alma Reubens in *The Clash.*

Jack Mulhall and Dorothy Mackaill in *Two Weeks Off* (1929).

———. "A Letter from Location." *Picture Play* (January 1925).

Sewell, Jameson. "And a Cockney Beauty." *Photoplay* (August 1923).

Percy Marmont

Barrett, E. E. "Personality Per Se." *Pictures and Picturegoer* (August 1928).

Breedlove, Frances. "Percy Marmont, a Reluctant Martyr." *Cinema Art* (December 1927).

Brownlow, Kevin. "Interview with Percy Marmont." *Amateur Movie Maker* (February 1960).

G. L. "The Progress of Percy Marmont." *Pictures and Picturegoer* (May 1921).

Landy, George. "They're Both Englishmen." *Photoplay* (November 1919).

Marmont, Percy. "Before I Forget." *Pictures and Picturegoer* (February 1931).

Selwyn, G. K. "Persecuting Percy." *Pictures and Picturegoer* (February 1925).

Service, Faith. "Living Down the Name of Percy." *Motion Picture Classic* (November 1919).

Slide, Anthony. "Percy Marmont's Hollywood." *The Silent Picture* (Summer 1970).

Steele, Charles Henry. "What a Leading Man Thinks About." *Picture Play* (October 1919).

Mae Marsh

Brooke, Frederick. "Two Snapshots of Mae Marsh." *Photoplay* (December 1914).
Bruce, Robert. "The Girl on the Cover." *Photoplay* (July 1915).
Cheatham, Maude. "The Marsh Flower." *Motion Picture Magazine* (February 1921).
Dunham, Harold. "Mae Marsh." *Films In Review* (June-July 1958). *See also* issues of October 1968 and March 1969.
————. "Mae Marsh, Robert Harron and D. W. Griffith." *The Silent Picture* (Autumn 1969).
Evans, Delight. "Will Mae Marsh Come Back?" *Picture Play* (March 1923).
Foley, Edna. "Have You Missed Her Too?" *Picture Play* (March 1920).

Mae Marsh and daughter, Mary.

Mae Marsh.

Kingsley, Grace. "Co-starring with the Sandman." *Picture Play* (September 1920).
Lederer, Josie P. "One Mae Day." *Pictures and Picturegoer* (September 1922).
Marsh, Mae. *Screen Acting.* Los Angeles: Photo-Star Publishing Company, 1921.
————. "What I Want To Do in My New Pictures." *Movie Weekly* (December 23, 1922).
Simpson, Hazel. "Too Many Marys Make a Mae." *Motion Picture Classic* (June 1918).
Smith, Frederick James. "Mae, Mary and Matrimony." *Motion Picture Classic* (March 1920).
Anonymous. "There Were Two Little Girls Named Mary." *Photoplay* (March 1917).
————. "Where Is Mae Marsh?" *Photoplay* (July 1919).
————. "Farewell Little Sister!" *Classic Film Collector* (Spring 1968).

May McAvoy

Bodeen, DeWitt. "May McAvoy." *Films In Review* (October 1968). *See also* issues of December 1968 and April 1969.
Evans, Delight. "Waiting for Fame." *Photoplay* (February 1921).

May McAvoy.

May McAvoy, Ramon Novarro, and Claire McDowell
in *Ben-Hur* (1925).

Goldbeck, Willis. "Shell-Rimmed Starlight." *Motion Picture Classic* (August 1921).

Hall, Gladys. "May In Miniature." *Motion Picture Magazine* (June 1921).

Jordan, Joan. "Peter Pan's Sister." *Photoplay* (November 1921).

Mahlon, Madeline. "Revolt a la McAvoy." *Photoplay* (April 1927).

McAvoy, May. "Comin' Up the Ladder." *Filmplay Journal* (September 1921).

McGregor, Malcolm. "May McAvoy." *Photoplay* (July 1924).

Naylor, Hazel Simpson. "The Poor Little Fame Girl." *Motion Picture Magazine* (January 1922).

Oettinger, Malcolm H. "Professor! Mendelssohn's 'Spring Song.'" *Picture Play* (January 1915).

Sangster, Margaret E. "The Enchanted Princess." *Photoplay* (April 1924).

Patsy Ruth Miller

Miller, Patsy Ruth. "As I See Myself." *Pictures and Picturegoer* (August 1927).

Moak, Bob. "What Her Father Paid for Stardom." *Picture Play* (October 1929).

Rogers St. Johns, Adela. "Presenting Patsy." *Photoplay* (October 1922).

Spensley, Dorothy. "Darn Those Engagements Says Patsy" *Photoplay* (December 1926).

Summers, Murray. "Patsy Ruth Miller." *Filmograph* (Winter 1971–Spring 1972).

Mary Miles Minter

Ames, Aydelott. "Mary Miles Minter." *Films In Review* (October 1969).

Patsy Ruth Miller adopts a patriotic pose.

Patsy Ruth Miller and Monte Blue in *So This Is Paris* (1926).

Astor, Truth. "Forget-Me-Not." *Motion Picture Classic* (August 1921).

Brewster, Eleanor. "Dire Influences of Dress on Mary Miles Minter." *Motion Picture Magazine* (March 1918).

Chapman, Ellen M. "Mary Miles Minter and Mother." *Motion Picture Classic* (August 1918).

Denton, Frances. "The Lonely Princess." *Photoplay* (June 1920).

Dixon, Jane. "What Happened to Mary?" *Photoplay* (February 1928).

Fletcher, Adele Whitely. "The Threshold." *Motion Picture Magazine* (May 1921).

Gatchell, Charles. "Concerning a Fairy Princess." *Picture Play* (March 1920).

Remont, Fritzi. "Those Shelby Girls." *Motion Picture Classic* (June 1919).

Thrall, Carl M. "Queen Mary." *Photoplay* (November 1915).

Wilson, B. F. "The Letters of Mary." *Motion Picture Classic* (August 1920).

Tom Mix

Cheatham, Maude. "The Darkest Hour." *Motion Picture Classic* (July 1922).

De Becker, Raymond. *De Tom Mix A James Dean*. Paris: Librairie Arthème Fayard, 1959.

Handy, Truman B. "Certainlee!" *Photoplay* (December 1919).

Kenrick, J. N. "Tom Mix Comes Back." *Pictures and Picturegoer* (April 30, 1932).

L. G. "Tom Mix and His Mother." *Pictures and Picturegoer* (January 1921).

Lincks, Peggy. "Tom Mixes In." *Motion Picture Magazine* (February 1919).

Mitchell, George, and Everson, William K. "Tom Mix." *Films in Review* (October, 1957).

Mix, Olive Stokes and Heath, Eric. *The Fabulous Tom Mix*. New Jersey: Prentice-Hall, 1957.

Mix, Tom. "Hunting with Roosevelt." *Photoplay World* (May 1919).

———. "My Life Story." *Photoplay* (February—April 1925).

———. "Sure You Can Make Money in California." *Photoplay* (September 1926).

———. "Romance and a Hard Boiled Shirt." *Photoplay* (January 1927).

———. "Wound Stripes of Hollywood." *Photoplay* (April 1927).

———. "Advice to Husbands and Wives." *Photoplay* (June 1927).

———. "The Vacation Complex." *Photoplay* (September 1927).

Mary Miles Minter reverses positions with her director Lloyd Ingraham.

Tom Mix.

————. "Wanted, Dead or Alive—Edmund Hoyle." *Photoplay* (December 1927).

————. "Making a Million." *Photoplay* (January-May 1928).

————. "The Loves of Tom Mix." *Photoplay* (March 1929).

————. "Shaking Hands with Death." *Pictures and Picturegoer* (November 26, 1932).

Montanye, Lillian. "The Riding Romeo." *Motion Picture Magazine* (October 1921).

Phillips, Malcolm. "Last of the Cowboy Kings." *Pictures and Picturegoer.* (November 2, 1940).

Remont, Fritzi. "Mixing in at Mixville." *Motion Picture Classic* (October 1919).

Roberts, P. Montgomery. "The Cowboy Beau Brummel." *Feature Movie Magazine* (March 1916).

St. Johns, Ivan. "A Chip off the Old Block." *Photoplay* (July 1925).

Tilley, Frank A. "On Location with Tom Mix." *Pictures and Picturegoer* (September 1923).

Colleen Moore.

Colleen Moore

Boone, Arabella. "One's Blue and One's Brown." *Photoplay* (February 1919).

Dening, Lynde. "Colleen Moore Interview." *The Film Forecast* (June 8, 1925).

Flint, Jerry. "The Most Amazing House in the World." *Photoplay* (May 1935).

Gassaway, Gordon. "Everybody's Little Sister." *Picture Play* (January 1920).

———. "With a Dash of Green." *Motion Picture Magazine* (June 1922).

Goodwins, Leslie. "What Might Have Been...." *Pictures and Picturegoer* (April 1921).

Howe, Herbert. "A Hollywood Girl." *Photoplay* (August 1922).

Moore, Colleen. "What Is Love?" *Photoplay* (November 1924).

———. Silent Star. New York: Doubleday, 1968.

Peltret, Elizabeth. "The Celtic Strain." *Motion Picture Classic* (July 1922).

Saurin, Clodagh. "The Wearing of the Green." *Photoplay* (March 1921).

Shelby, Hazel. "The Young Veteran." *Motion Picture Classic* (January 1921).

Smith, Frederick James. "The Unsophisticated Colleen." *Motion Picture Magazine* (June 1921).

Spears, Jack. "Colleen Moore." *Films In Review* (August—September 1963).

Spensley, Dorothy. "The Cinderella Girl." *Photoplay* (August 1926).

Stern, Harold. "Colleen Moore: The First of the Flappers Is Still Going Strong." *After Dark* (October 1968).

Ussher, Kathleen. "Sausages and Sauerkraut!" *Pictures and Picturegoer* (August 1927).

Anonymous. "A Captivating Colleen." *Pictures and Picturegoer* (October 1924).

———. "A Bob Each Way." *Pictures and Picturegoer* (January 1928).

Colleen Moore and Jack Mulhall in *Orchids and Ermine* (1927).

James Morrison

Pollock, Arthur. "James Morrison on the Tricks of the Screen Actor's Trade." *Motion Picture Magazine* (November 1916).

Scott, Dorothy. "A Tip for Pershing." *Photoplay* (June 1918).

Anonymous. "Brief Biographies of Popular Players." *Motion Picture Magazine* (February 1915).

———. "Chats with the Players." *Motion Picture Magazine* (October 1915).

———. "Jimmy Morrison, Versatile Vitagrapher." *Moving Picture World* (May 6, 1916).

Jack Mulhall

Cheatham, Maude. "Because of a Dress Suit." *Motion Picture Magazine* (June 1921).

Drew, Robert. "Once the Gibson Man." *Motion Picture Magazine* (April 1922).

Elliott, Malcolm. "The Youngest Grand Old Man!" *Photoplay* (November 1930).

James Morrison.

Larkin, Mar. "The Pose-Killer." *Photoplay* (November 1928).

Peltret, Elizabeth. "The Romantic Irish." *Motion Picture Magazine* (July 1920).

Anonymous. "Jack Mulhall of New York." *Moving Picture World* (April 7, 1917).

Mae Murray

Ardmore, Jane. *The Self-Enchanted.* New York: McGraw-Hill, 1959.

Bennett, Alice. "Mae Murray Makes Believe." *Motion Picture Magazine* (February 1919).

Briscoe, Johnson. "A Child of Fortune." *Motion Picture Magazine* (March 1917).

Corliss, Allen. "Motoring with Mae." *Photoplay* (March 1917).

Evans, Delight. "The Truth about Mae Murray." *Photoplay* (August 1920).

Hall, Alice. "The Butterfly on the Reel." *Pictures and Picturegoer* (September 1921).

Lee, Carol. "A Bit of Fluff from Folly-Land." *Motion Picture Classic* (June 1917).

Lusk, Norbert. "She Knows What We Want." *Picture Play* (September 1923).

Minton, Eric. "Mae Murray, Star." *Filmograph* (Vol. 1, No. 3).

Morgan, Mary. "Secrets of Mae Murray's Success." *Photoplay* (January 1922).

Murray, Mae. "The Milky Way to Beauty." *Photoplay* (November 1925).

Rogers St. Johns, Adela. "Mae Murray — A Study in Contradictions." *Photoplay* (July 1924).

Sayford, I. S. "Talking All around Mae." *Photoplay* (October 1916).

West, Myrtle. "The Price They Paid for Stardom." *Photoplay* (November 1926).

Anonymous. "Mae Murray—the Adorable." *Moving Picture World* (September 8, 1917).

———. "Mae Murray—the Star Who Danced to Fame." *Theatre* (June 1919).

———. "The 'Murray' Widow." *Pictures and Picturegoer* (September 1925).

Conrad Nagel

Albert, Katherine. "The Strange Case of Conrad Nagel." *Photoplay* (September 1930).

Allison, Dorothy. "Conrad in Quest of Age." *Photoplay* (July 1919).

Cheatham, Maude. "Conrad in Quest of Adventure." *Motion Picture Magazine* (March 1922).

Kingsley, Grace. "Conrad Nagel At Home." *Pictures*

Mae Murray.

Conrad Nagel, circa 1920.

and Picturegoer (February 1925).

Larkin, Mark. "Conrad in Quest of a Voice." Photoplay (January 1929).

Lowell, Alexander. "Behind the Scenes." Motion Picture Magazine (August 1919).

Lyle, Frank. "An Untold Romance of the Movies." Filmplay Journal (September 1921).

Nagel, Conrad. "What Is Wrong with the Movies." Pictures and Picturegoer (April 8, 1933).

Peltret, Elizabeth. "The Convictions of Conrad." Motion Picture Classic (October 1920).

Sherwood, C. Blythe. "Emergency Nagel." Motion Picture Classic (March 1919).

Smith, B. Henry. "The Secret of the Submarine Kiss." Picture Play (August 1920).

Spensley, Dorothy. "Too Good To Be True." Photoplay (February 1927).

Sweet, Blanche. "Conrad Nagel." Photoplay (June 1924).

Trepel, Beth. "The Importance of Being Earnest." Motion Picture Magazine (March 1921).

Alla Nazimova

Fredericks, Edwin. "The Real Nazimova." Photoplay (February 1920).

Gray, Frances. "Nazimova and Her Language of the Soul." Motion Picture Magazine (October 1920).

Hall, Gladys and Fletcher, Adele Whitely. "We Interview Camille." Motion Picture Magazine (January 1922).

Howe, Herbert. "Nazimova Speaks." Picture Play (September 1920).

———. "The Real Nazimova." Pictures and Picturegoer (January 1921).

———. "A Misunderstood Woman." Photoplay (April 1922).

———. "A Darling of Salome." Photoplay (March 1923).

Kirkland, Alexander. "The Woman from Yalta." Theatre Arts (December 1949).

K. U. "The Real Nazimova." Pictures and Picturegoer (July 1927).

Landa, Gertrude. "When Nazimova Failed." Pictures and Picturegoer (March 1921).

Montanye, Lillian. "A Half Hour with Nazimova." Motion Picture Classic (July 1917).

Naylor, Hazel Simpson. "My Devilish Ambition." Motion Picture Magazine (July 1918).

Old Timer, An. "Before They Were Stars: Nazimova." New York Dramatic Mirror (March 27, 1920).

Rogers St. Johns, Adela. "Temperament? Certainly Says Nazimova." Photoplay (October 1926).

Service, Faith. "Memoirs of Madame." Motion Picture Classic (November 1922).

Thompson, E. R. "The Art of Alla Nazimova." Pictures and Picturegoer (January 1925).

Wilkes, W. Ernest. "Alla Nazimova." Photoplay World (July 1919).

Alla Nazimova and Rudolph Valentino in Camille (1921).

Pola Negri

Allvine, Glendon. "How Polish Is Pola?" *Filmplay Journal* (June 1922).

Bodeen, DeWitt and Gene Ringgold. "Pola Negri." *Screen Facts* (No. 15).

Carr, Harry. "The Mystery of Pola Negri." *Motion Picture Magazine* (April 1925).

Frazer, Robert. "Pola Negri." *Photoplay* (July 1924).

Hall, Leonard. "The Passing of Pola." *Photoplay* (December 1928).

Haskins, Harrison. "Who Is Pola Negri?" *Motion Picture Classic* (February 1921).

Howe, Herbert. "The Real Pola Negri." *Photoplay* (November 1922).

———. "The Loves of Pola Negri." *Photoplay* (November 1923).

Jordan, Joan. "You Can't Hurry Pola." *Photoplay* (March 1923).

Lyon, Ben. "Vampires I Have Known." *Photoplay* (February 1925).

Mortimer, Reg. "With Pola in Paris." *Pictures and Picturegoer* (January 1929).

———. "Welcome Back, Pola and Passion." *Pictures and Picturegoer* (February 6, 1932).

Negri, Pola. "The Autobiography of Pola Negri." *Photoplay* (January—April 1924).

———. "Robert W. Frazer." *Photoplay* (June 1924).

———. "What Is Love?" *Photoplay* (November 1924).

———. "I Become Converted to the Happy Ending." *Motion Picture Director* (March 1926).

———. "My Ideal Screen Lover." *Pictures and Picturegoer* (March 1931).

———. *Memoirs of a Star*. New York: Doubleday, 1970.

———. *La Vie Et La Reve Au Cinema*. Paris: Albin Michel, undated.

Pryor, Nancy. "Pola Comes Back to Hollywood."

Pola Negri in *A Woman of the World* (1925).

Motion Picture Magazine (August 1931).

Shulsinger, Rose. "The Uncertainty of Certainty." *Motion Picture Classic* (October 1922).

Simpson, Grace. "The Magnetic Pole." *Pictures and Picturegoer* (August 1928).

St. Johns, Ivan. "How Pola Was Tamed." *Photoplay* (January 1926).

Teeman, Lawrence. "Star of Yesterday." *Players Showcase* (Fall 1965).

Tully, Jim. "Pola Negri." *Vanity Fair* (August 1926).

Vallentin, Antonina. "Film Stars in Germany." *Shadowland* (February 1921).

Vinder, Maximilian. "She Delivered the Goods." *Photoplay* (May 1922).

York, Cal. "He Who Got Slapped and Why." *Photoplay* (July 1926).

Anonymous. "Pola from Poland." *Pictures and Picturegoer* (January 1923).

Anna Q. Nilsson

Courtlandt, Roberta. "Play Days of Anna." *Motion Picture Classic* (April 1917).

Delvigne, Doris. "The Intimate Doings of Anna Q." *Motion Picture Magazine* (September 1919).

Fletcher, Adele Whitely. "Cerise Pajamas and Antiques." *Motion Picture Magazine* (August 1921).

———. "Beauty, Brains or Luck?" *Photoplay* (October 1930).

Lonergan, Elizabeth. "My Impressions of London." *Pictures and Picturegoer* (March 1925).

Mahlon, Madeline. "On with the Pants." *Photoplay* (July 1926).

O'Reilly, Edward S. "A Misplaced Interview." *Photoplay* (November 1920).

Phillips, Gwen. "Anna Q. Nilsson, a Swedish Beauty Well Known on the Screen." *Photodrama* (September 1921).

Rogers St. Johns, Adela. "At Last—the Blonde Vamp." *Photoplay* (March 1925).

———. "Where Is Anna Q?" *The New Movie Magazine* (September 1930).

Spensley, Dorothy. "Why 6 Marriages Failed." *Photoplay* (May 1930).

Tully, Jim. "Anna Q. Nilsson." *Vanity Fair* (September 1926).

Anonymous. "Anna Q. Nilsson: A Brief Biography." *Pictures and Picturegoer* (December 1, 1917).

Mabel Normand

Bartlett, Randolph. "Why Aren't We Killed?" *Photoplay* (April 1916).

Anna Q. Nilsson.

———. "Would You Ever Suspect It?" *Photoplay* (August 1918).

Codd, Elsie. "Seeing Limehouse with Mabel." *Pictures and Picturegoer* (September 1922).

Gaddis, Pearl. "The Dream That Came True." *Motion Picture Magazine* (December 1916).

Goldbeck, Willis. "Worldy, but Not Weary." *Motion Picture Magazine* (September 1921).

Howe, Herbert. "The Diaries of Mabel Normand." *Pantomime* (October 12, 1921).

Lusk, Norbert. "The Girl on the Cover." *Picture Play* (February 1918).

Old Timer, An. "Before They Were Stars: Mabel Normand." *New York Dramatic Mirror* (March 20, 1920).

Peeples, Samuel. "Madcap." *Classic Film Collector* (Spring—Summer 1970).

Quirk, James R. "The Girl on the Cover." *Photoplay* (August 1915).

———. "Mabel Normand Says Goodbye." *Photoplay* (May 1930).

Rex, Will. "Behind the Scenes with Fatty and Mabel." *Picture Play* (April 1916).

Rogers St. Johns, Adela. "Hello Mabel!" *Photoplay* (August 1921).

Roscoe "Fatty" Arbuckle and Mabel Normand in *He Did and He Didn't* (1916).

———. "The Butterfly Man and the Little Clown." *Photoplay* (July 1929).

Smith, Frederick James. "Mabel in a Hurry." *Motion Picture Magazine* (November 1918).

Anonymous. "Mabel Normand." *Moving Picture World* (July 11, 1914).

———. "Storms, Chocolate Cakes, and Vampires Delight Her." *Pictures and Picturegoer* (August 24, 1918).

Jane Novak

Fullbright, Tom. "The Films of Jane Novak." *Classic Film Collector* (Spring 1968–Spring 1969).

Gassaway, Gordon. "The 'Punch-the-Clock' Girl." *Motion Picture Magazine* (April 1922).

Handy, Truman B. "Little Sister, Huh!" *Motion Picture Classic* (July 1920).

Howe, Selma. "The Star of the Doll's House." *Picture Play* (April 1920).

McKelvie, Martha Groves. "Just Jane." *Motion Picture Magazine* (October 1918).

Slide, Anthony. "Jane Novak Interview." *The Silent Picture* (Spring 1972).

Winship, Mary. "That Chin." *Photoplay* (January 1922).

Jane Novak.

Ramon Novarro

Albert, Katherine. "The Volunteer Grandma." *Photoplay* (April 1930).

Biery, Ruth. "Why Ramon Novarro Decided To Remain in the Movies." *Photoplay* (October 1928).

Bodeen, DeWitt. "Ramon Novarro." *Films In Review* (November 1967). *See also* issue of December 1967.

———. "Ramon Novarro." *The Silent Picture.* (Summer 1969).

Chute, Margaret. "So This Is Ramon Novarro." *Pictures and Picturegoer* (April 23, 1932).

D'Arne, Wilson. "Novarro Comes Back." *Pictures and Picturegoer* (October 30, 1937).

E. L. "Enter Roman Novarro." *Pictures and Picturegoer* (May 1923).

Hounder, Silas. "Ramon and Pythias." *Pictures and Picturegoer* (December 1924).

Howe, Herbert. "What Are Matinee Idols Made Of?" *Photoplay* (April 1923).

———. "A Prediction." *Photoplay* (May 1924).

———. "Ramon Novarro in Europe." *Photoplay* (April 1925).

La Due Dane. "A Kinema Chameleon." *Pictures and Picturegoer* (November 1925).

Lasky, Betty. "Star of Yesterday." *Players Showcase* (Summer 1965).

Lonergan, Elizabeth. "Ramon's Own Theatre." *Pictures and Picturegoer* (September 1928).

Novarro, Ramon. "Alice Terry." *Photoplay* (July 1924).

———. "My Eleven Years of Stardom." *Pictures and Picturegoer* (July 1, 1933).

Reyes, Manuel. "Ramon's Ancestors Greet the Mayflower." *Photoplay* (October 1925).

Terry, Alice. "Ramon Novarro." *Photoplay* (July 1924).

Anonymous. "Mexican Emigrant Makes Good." *Pictures and Picturegoer* (September 8, 1934).

———. "Rex Ingram and Stardom." *Pictures and Picturegoer* (September 15, 1934).

Jean Paige

Fletcher, Adele Whitely. "Sick-a-Bed-Lady." *Motion Picture Magazine* (April–May 1920).

———. "Nee Jean Paige." *Motion Picture Magazine* (June 1921).

Forthe, Walter. "Of the Sub-Deb Squad." *Photoplay* (December 1919).

Ramon Novarro was best man at the wedding of composer Percy Grainger and painter Ella Viola Strom during a symphony concert at the Hollywood Bowl.

James Morrison and Jean Paige in *Black Beauty* (1921).

J.L. "Three Pages." *Pictures and Picturegoer* (August 1922).

Kruh, Regina B. "Jean Paige Tells Us What She Loves Best." *Photo-Play Journal* (February 1919).

———. "The O'Henry Dream Girl." *Photo-Play World* (July 1919).

Mary Philbin

Hounder, Silas. "Little Mary Philbin." *Pictures and Picturegoer* (September 1924).

Littlefield, Constance P. "The Hand of Destiny." *Picture Play* (June 1925).

Smith, Agnes. "Mary Herself." *Photoplay* (November 1926).

St. Johns, Ivan. "The Girl on the Cover." *Photoplay* (October 1924).

Mary Pickford

Arnold, H. "Mary Pickford Says, 'I Am My Own Boss.'" *Pictures and Picturegoer* (August 27, 1932).

Mary Pickford in *The Little American* (1917).

Mary Philbin, as Dea, in *The Man Who Laughs* (1927).

Bates, Billy. "The Pickford-Fairbanks Wooing." *Photoplay* (June 1920).

Belasco, David. "When Mary Pickford Came to Me." *Photoplay* (December 1915).

Bent, Martin J. "The House That Mary Built." *Picture Play* (June 1920).

Birdwell, Russell J. "When I Am Old, as Told by Mary Pickford." *Photoplay* (February 1925).

Blaisdell, George F. "'Little Mary' and Her Correspondents." *Moving Picture World* (July 18, 1914).

Breen, Max "She Was the World's Sweetheart and Now—" *Pictures and Picturegoer* (April 3, 1937).

Card, James. "The Films of Mary Pickford." *Image* (December 1959).

Cheatham, Maude S. "On Location with Mary Pickford." *Motion Picture Magazine* (June 1919).

Cushman, Robert B. *Tribute to Mary Pickford.* Washington: American Film Institute, 1970.

Donnell, Dorothy. "Mary Pickford Lives for Today." *Motion Picture Magazine* (February 1936).

Dudley, Fredda. "One Mary in a Million!" *Movieland* (August 1945).

Edwards, Leo. "The Incomparable Mary." *Feature Movie Magazine* (October 10, 1915).

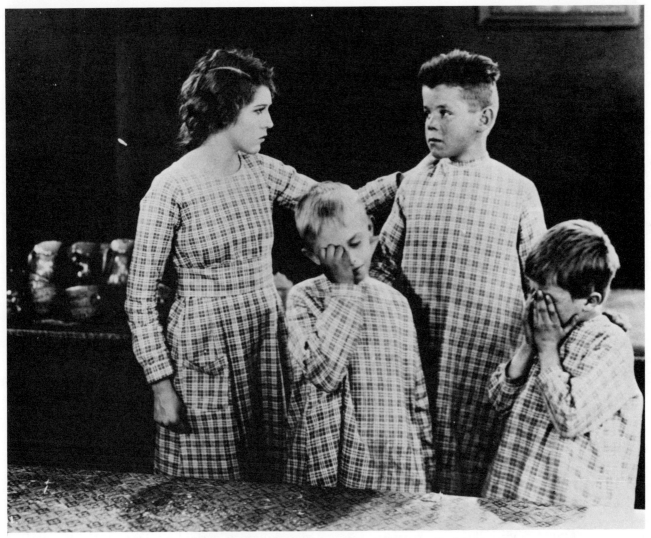

Mary Pickford and the orphan children in *Daddy Long Legs* (1919).

Evans, Delight. "Mary Pickford, the Girl." *Motion Picture Magazine* (July 1918).

Fletcher, Adele Whitely. "Mary." *Motion Picture Magazine* (June 1922).

Hall, Gladys and Adele Whitely Fletcher. "As They Were." *Motion Picture Magazine* (November 1920).

Hall, Gladys. "Mary Pickford's Own Story." *Pictures and Picturegoer* (March 17, 1934).

Hall, Leonard. "How about Mary and Doug?" *Photoplay* (August 1930).

Harriman, Mary Case. "Sweetheart." *New Yorker* (April 7, 1934).

Howe, Herbert. "Mary Pickford's Favorite Stars and Films." *Photoplay* (January 1924).

———. "Mary Pickford's Greatest Love." *Filmplay Journal* (September 1921).

Johnson, Julian. "Mary Pickford, Herself and Her Career." *Photoplay* (November 1915–February 1916).

Kegler, Estelle. "The Charm of Wistfulness." *Photoplay* (August 1913).

Larkin, Mark. "The Mother of Mary." *Motion Picture Magazine* (September 1919).

Lasky, Betty. "America's Sweetheart—Mary Pickford." *Players Showcase* (Winter 1966).

Lederer, Josie M. "The Persistent Honeymooners." *Pictures and Picturegoer* (January 1922).

Lee, Raymond. *The Films of Mary Pickford.* South Brunswick and New York: A.S. Barnes, 1970.

McKelvie, Martha Groves. "Surely It Can't Be Mary." *Motion Picture Classic* (July 1918).

Meehan, Jeanette. "Why Mary Pickford Won't Retire." *Pictures and Picturegoer* (December 14, 1935).

Mercer, Janet. "The Fairbanks Social War Is On!" *Photoplay* (August 1936).

Niver, Kemp N. *Mary Pickford: Comedienne.* Los Angeles: Locare, 1969.

O'Higgins, Harvey. "To What Green Altar." *New Republic* (February 15, 1919).

P. B. "Lettre de Paris sur Mary Pickford." *Cahiers Du Cinema* (September 1966).

Pickford, Mary. "What It Means To Be a Movie Actress." *Ladies Home Journal* (January 1915).

———. "The Body in the Bosphorus." *Theatre* (April 1919).

———. *Pickfordisms For Success.* Los Angeles: Photoplay Research Society, 1922.

———"Greatest Business in the World." *Collier's* (June 10, 1922).

———. "Mary Is Looking for Pictures." *Photoplay* (June 1925).

———. "Mary Pickford Awards." *Photoplay* (October 1925).

———. "My Rendezvous with Life." New York: H.C. Kinsey, 1935.

———. *Sunshine and Shadow.* London: William Heinemann, 1956.

Ponder, Jack. "A Day with Mary Pickford." *Pictures and Picturegoer* (June 1929).

Rogers St. Johns, Adela. "Why Does the World Love Mary?" *Photoplay* (December 1921).

———. "The Story of the Married Life of Doug and Mary." *Photoplay* (February 1927).

———. "Why Mary Pickford Bobbed Her Hair." *Photoplay* (September 1928).

Russell, M. Lewis. "Mary Pickford—Director." *Photoplay* (March 1920).

Sanderson, Peter. "Studio Actors Knit with Mary Pickford." *Motion Picture Magazine* (April 1918).

Sangster, Margaret E. "Mary Pickford's Search for Happiness." *Photoplay* (February 1935.)

Scaramazza, Paul A. "Rediscovering Mary Pickford." *Film Fan Monthly* (December 1970).

Smith, Alison. "Owen Talks about Mary." *Photoplay* (December 1919).

Smith, Frederick James. "Mary Had a Little Tear." *Motion Picture Classic* (September 1917).

Spears, Jack. "Mary Pickford's Directors." *Films In Review* (February 1966).

Synon, Katherine. "The Unspoiled Mary Pickford." *Photoplay* (September 1914).

Whitaker, Alma. "Mrs. Douglas Fairbanks Analyzes Mary Pickford." *Photoplay* (March 1928).

Wright, Edna. "A Week-end with Mary Pickford." *Photoplay* (March 1915).

———. "Mary Pickford Plus 'Silent Money Talk.'"

Motion Picture Classic (March 1917).

Anonymous. "Has Mary Pickford Retired." *Photoplay* (October 1918).

———. "Special Mary Pickford Number." *Pictures and Picturegoer* (June 14, 1919).

———. "America's Sweetheart Yesterday and Tomorrow." *Motion Picture Director* (February 1926).

———. "Mary in Spite of Herself." *Pictures and Picturegoer* (September 1926).

———. "The Future of Mary and Doug." *Pictures and Picturegoer* (May 7, 1932).

Esther Ralston

E. E. B. "Esther Ralston, the Girl on the Cover." *Pictures and Picturegoer* (October 1929).

Hughes, Miriam. "Gone—Another Ingenue." *Photoplay* (January 1931).

Ralston, Esther. "Should Film Stars Marry." *Pictures and Picturegoer* (November 12, 1932).

St. Johns, Ivan. "Peter Pan's Mother." *Photoplay* (April 1925).

Waterbury, Ruth. "Love and Esther Ralston." *Photoplay* (October 1926).

Charles Ray

Bodeen, DeWitt. "Charles Ray." *Films In Review* (November 1968).

Cheatham, Maude. "The Bashful Boy." *Motion Picture Classic* (July 1921).

Grier, Arline. "Charles Ray." *Photo-Play World* (July 1919).

Esther Ralston with Dorothy Arzner, her director on *Fashions for Women* (1927).

Charles Ray.

Hall, Gladys and Fletcher Adele Whitely. "We Interview Charles Ray." *Motion Picture Magazine* (March 1922).

Martin, Minerva. "The Young and Debonair Charles Ray." *Photoplay* (October 1914).

Naylor, Hazel Simpson. "Keeping the Ray Focused." *Motion Picture Magazine* (January 1920).

Porter, Katherine Anne. "The Real Ray." *Motion Picture Magazine* (October 1920).

Ray, Charles. "I Spent a Million To Dress Up." *Photoplay* (September 1917).

Remont, Fritzi. "Taking an X-Ray of Charles." *Motion Picture Magazine* (September 1918).

Rogers St. Johns, Adela. "Don't Cheat Your Sweetheart." *Photoplay* (December 1919).

Ussher, Kathleen. "Re-enter Charles Ray." *Pictures and Picturegoer* (October 1926).

Anonymous. "Charles Ray—a Power on the Screen." *Pictures and Picturegoer* (September 2, 1916).

Wallace Reid

Allen, Pauline. "Keeping in Training for the Strenuous Life." *Motion Picture Classic* (December 1916).

Bodeen, DeWitt. "Wallace Reid." *Films In Review* (April 1966). *See also* issues of May, June—July, and August—September 1966 and June—July 1967.

Boone, Arabella. "Father of the Sport Shirt." *Photoplay* (November 1919).

Carter, Charles. "Some Family Skeletons of Filmdom." *Picture Play* (February 1921).

Cheatham, Maude S. "Wally, the Genial." *Motion Picture Magazine* (October 1920).

Codd, Elsie. "Behind the Screen with Wallace Reid." *Pictures and Picturegoer* (February 1921).

Gassaway, Gordon. "What It Costs To Be A Star." *Picture Play* (February 1922).

Hall, Gladys and Fletcher, Adele Whitely. "We Interview Wally." *Motion Picture Magazine* (September 1921).

Handy, Truman B. "Anatol Himself." *Motion Picture Magazine* (August 1922).

Howe, Herbert. "The Unhappy Ending of Wallace Reid's Life Story." *Photoplay* (March 1923).

Manners, Marjory. "The Home That Wally Built." *Picture Play* (August 1918).

Movie Margerie. "Dare-Devil Wally." *Pictures and Picturegoer* (March 1, 1919).

McGaffey, Kenneth. "Wandering with Wally." *Photoplay* (June 1918).

Naylor, Hazel Simpson. "Once upon a Time, or Wally Reid in a Reminiscent Mood." *Motion Picture Classic* (April 1918).

Peltret, Elizabeth. "Girls I Have Made Love To." *Motion Picture Magazine* (September 1919).

Reid, Bertha W. "My Boy Wallace." *Filmplay Journal* (September 1921).

———. "Memories of Wallace Reid by His Mother." *Pictures and Picturegoer* (March 1924).

———. *Wallace Reid: His Life Story*. Los Angeles: Sorg, 1923.

Reid, Wallace. "How I Got In." *Motion Picture Magazine* (January 1918).

———. "How To Hold a Wife." *Photoplay* (January 1921).

———. "A Week with the Stars: Thursday." *Photoplay* (November 1921).

Reid, Mrs. Wallace. "Coming Back at Friend's Husband." *Photoplay* (November 1921).

———. "Wally." *Pictures and Picturegoer* (October 1922).

———. "The Real Wally." *Photoplay* (March 1925).

Rex, Will. "Romance of the Studios." *Picture Play* (July 1916).

Sands, Ethel. "A Fan's Adventures in Hollywood." *Picture Play* (March 1922).

Schallert, Edwin. "Have You a Guiding Star." *Picture Play* (November 1922).

Shelley, Hazel. "Ideals of an Idol." *Motion Picture*

Wallace Reid.

Classic (March 1921).

Van Vranken, Frederick. "That Indescribable Something." *Motion Picture Magazine* (September 1922).

Wardell, Eleanor. "Wallace Reid at Home." *Motion Picture Magazine* (February 1917).

Waterbury, Ruth. "The Final Fade-Out." *Photoplay* (March 1926).

Woodridge, A. L. "Phantom Daddies of the Screen." *Photoplay* (January 1934).

York, Scollard. "Wally the Wonderful." *Photoplay* (March 1916).

Anonymous. "Wallace Reid." *Moving Picture World* (October 23, 1915).

———. "The Man Who Has Everything." *Pictures and Picturegoer* (June 1922).

Billie Rhodes

Hall, Helene. "A Sweet Girl Graduate." *Photoplay World* (May 1919).

Peltret, Elizabeth. "Billie Rhodes—Circus Girl." *Motion Picture Classic* (January 1919).

Ruth Roland.

Ruth Roland

Bruner, Frank V. "Along Came Ruth." *Motion Picture Classic* (July 1919).

Gebhart, Myrtle. "The Real Ruth Roland." *Picture Play* (December 1926).

Goldbeck, Willis. "The Primitive." *Motion Picture Magazine* (December 1921).

Groves, Gloria. "A Real Vaudeville Equilibrist." *Photoplay* (April 1919).

Hall, Alice. "Roughing It with Ruth Roland." *Pictures and Picturegoer* (June 1921).

Peterson, Elizabeth. "Comrade Ruth." *Motion Picture Classic* (April 1917).

Rogers St. Johns, Adela. "Just a Good Business Man." *Photoplay* (August 1922).

Roland, Ruth. "Personality in Dress." *Photoplay* (June 1915).

———. "Why I'm in Serials." *Pantomime* (December 10, 1921).

———. "Ruth's New Role." *Pictures and Picturegoer* (June 1923).

———. "Revelations of Ruth Roland." *Pictures and Picturegoer* (January 1927).

Smith, Frank Leon. "Pearl White and Ruth Roland." *Films In Review* (December 1960).

Anonymous. "Miss Ruth Roland." *Moving Picture World* (March 7, 1914).

———. "Ruth Roland." *Moving Picture World* (July 11, 1914).

———. "A New Kalem Star." *Moving Picture World* (December 5, 1914).

———. "Ruth Roland." *Moving Picture World* (July 24, 1915).

———. "Ruth Roland Up-to-Date." *Pictures and Picturegoer* (October 27, 1917).

Alma Rubens

Howe, Herbert. "Meet the Duchess!" *Photoplay* (July 1923).

Jameson, Charles. "Alma Reuben: Business Woman." *Motion Picture Classic* (July 1919).

Kipling, Lilian Mae. "Alma Rubens." *Photoplay World* (July 1919).

Lamb, Grace. "Youth Speaking." *Motion Picture Magazine* (August 1920).

Montanye, Lillian. "West Is East." *Motion Picture Magazine* (March 1920).

Rubens, Alma. "Lewis Stone." *Photoplay* (June 1924).

Anonymous. "Of the Younger Set." *Photoplay* (April 1917).

———. "Alma Rubens—a Red Rose in an Onyx Vase." *Motion Picture Classic* (August 1918).

Alma Reubens.

Larry Semon

Gentz, Will T. "A Cartoonist Turned Comedian." *Photo-play World* (June 1919).
Karl, Peter. "The Message of Larry Semon." *Positif* (June 1969).
Anonymous. "Simple Semon." *Pictures and Picturegoer* (May 1925).

Clarine Seymour

Haskins, Harrison. "The Last Interview." *Motion Picture Classic* (July 1920).
Peltret, Elizabeth. "Introducing Cutie Beautiful." *Motion Picture Classic* (July 1919).
Robbins, E. M. "The Two Strange Women." *Photoplay* (August 1919).
Shannon, Betty. "An Unfinished Story." *Photoplay* (July 1920).

Clarine Seymour (left) in *Scarlet Days* (1919).

Larry Semon.

Norma Shearer

Baskette, Kirtley. "A Queen Comes Back." *Photoplay* (July 1938).

Burke, Randolph Carroll. "She Smiled Her Way to Success." *Pictures and Picturegoer* (June 13, 1931).

Cruikshank, Herbert. "Shearer Nerve." *Talking Screen* (January 1930).

Fletcher, Adele Whitely. "Beauty, Brains or Luck?" *Photoplay* (August 1930).

Hayes, Barbara. "The Man Who Guides Norma Shearer's Fatherless Children." *Photoplay* (November 1937).

Howe, Herbert. "What Is Norma Shearer's Charm for Men." *Photoplay* (August 1930).

Jacobs, Jack. "Norma Shearer." *Films In Review* (August–September 1960). *See also* issue of October 1960.

Lathem, Maude. "Norma Shearer's Personal Revelations." *Pictures and Picturegoer* (February 10, 1934).

Lee, Basil. "The Real First Lady of Films." *Photoplay* (July 1934).

Manners, Dorothy. "How Norma Shearer Faces the Future." *Photoplay* (December 1936).

Ogden, Elaine. "Will Norma Shearer Retire?" *Photoplay* (August 1930).

An unusual photograph of Norma Shearer in *Lady of the Night* (1925).

Ramon Novarro and Norma Shearer in *The Student Prince* (1927).

Parker, Eleanor. "Norma Shearer's Secret of Success." *Pictures and Picturegoer* (August 20, 1933).

Parsons, Harriet. "Norma Talks about Joan." *Pictures and Picturegoer* (March 25, 1933).

Rankin, Ruth. "They're All Queening It." *Photoplay* (December 1933).

Rogers St. Johns, Adela. "I'm Not Going To Marry Says Norma Shearer." *Photoplay* (May 1927).

Shearer, Norma. "I'm Tame as a Lion." *American Magazine* (July 1935).

Sheppard, Ruth. "Hollywood's Biggest Comeback." *Photoplay* (November 1957).

Tully, Jim. "Early Struggles of Norma Shearer." *Pictures and Picturegoer* (August 17, 1935).

———. "She Made Herself a Star." *Pictures and Picturegoer* (October 19, 1935).

Willson, Dixie. "Norma Shearer's Handful of Memories." *Photoplay* (October 1938).

Zeitlin, Ida. "Norma Shearer Talks about *Romeo and Juliet*." *Motion Picture Magazine* (October 1936).

Anita Stewart

Anita Stewart.

Bodeen, DeWitt. "Anita Stewart." *Films In Review* (March 1968). *See also* issue of June–July 1968.

Crane, Beverly. "Anita Stewart Vacationing at Her Summer Home on Long Island." *Movie Weekly* (August 27, 1921).

Ettinger, Margaret. "Just What Is Stardom?" *Picture Play* (September 1923).

Evans, Elizabeth. "A Stradivarius of the Screen." *Motion Picture Classic* (July 1919).

Goldbeck, Willis. "The Star at Evening." *Motion Picture Classic* (July 1921).

———. "Human Stuff." *Motion Picture Magazine* (June 1922).

Hall, Gladys. "Ex-tra! The Story of Anita Stewart's Hoodoo Year, as Told for the First Time." *Motion Picture Magazine* (August 1928).

Handy, Truman B. "Anita's Ambitions." *Motion Picture Magazine* (April–May 1920).

———. "The Ambitions of Anita." *Pictures and Picturegoer* (September 1921).

Johnson, Julian. "Anita: A Star-in-Law." *Photoplay* (April 1915).

———. "The Girl on the Cover." *Photoplay* (September 1915).

Lachmund, Marjorie Gleyre. "Sweet Anita." *Motion Picture Magazine* (April 1917).

Martin, Peter. "Twilight Talk." *Motion Picture Magazine* (October 1921).

Old Timer, An. "Before They Were Stars: Anita Stewart." *New York Dramatic Mirror* (April 24, 1920).

Rogers St. Johns, Adela. "A Pair of Queens." *Photoplay* (September 1919).

Anonymous. "Pretty Anita Stewart." *Feature Movie Magazine* (June 1916).

———. "Anita—Not a Neater!" *Pictures and Picturegoer* (September 23, 1916).

Gloria Swanson

Albert, Katherine. "What Next for Gloria?" *Photoplay* (July 1929).

Ashley, Renita. "Almost Changed the City's Name to Swanson, W. Va." *Photoplay* (November 1925).

Blair, Duncan. "Evening of a Great Star." *Pictures and Picturegoer* (July 22, 1950).

Bodeen, DeWitt. "Gloria Swanson." *Films In Review* (April 1965). *See also* issues of August–September and October 1965 and December 1967.

Breen, Max. "Glamorous Gloria." *Pictures and Picturegoer* (May 29, 1937).

Brownlow, Kevin. "Gloria Swanson." *Film* (No. 41).

Collier, Marjory. "Glorifying the Mother-Woman." *Pictures and Picturegoer* (March 1930).

Deeter, Grace. "The Glory of Gloria." *Photoplay World* (June 1919).

Gloria Swanson.

Elland, Edyth. "Gloria." *Pictures and Picturegoer* (September 1924).

Evans, Delight. "Don't Change Your Coiffure." *Photoplay* (August 1919).

Fletcher, Adele Whitely. "Instead of the Silken Gloria." *Motion Picture Magazine* (December 1921).

———. "Beauty, Brains or Luck?" *Photoplay* (August 1930).

———. "What Next, Gloria?" *Movie Mirror* (December 1931).

Forlow, Robert. "The Glamor of Gloria." *Pictures and Picturegoer* (November 1927).

Gassaway, Gordon. "Gloria, the Occult." *Picture Play* (July 1920).

Glyn, Elinor. "Gloria Swanson as a Mother." *Pictures and Picturegoer* (August 13, 1932).

Goldbeck, Willis. "Gossamer." *Motion Picture Classic* (October 1921).

Hudson, Richard and Lee, Ray. *Gloria Swanson.* South Brunswick and New York: A. S. Barnes and Company, 1970.

Hyland, Dic. "Won by a Nose." *Photoplay* (November 1928).

Keel, Chester. "What Next Gloria." *Photoplay* (April 1925).

Keen, Eliot. "Gloria Passes the Test." *Screenland* (January 1927).

Lang, Harry. "So This Is Gloria!" *Photoplay* (September 1930).

Lyon, Ben. "Vampires I Have Known." *Photoplay* (February 1930).

Mastin, Mildred. "The Husbands in Gloria's Career." *Photoplay* (July 1934).

Morgan, Anne. "Gloria Swanson and Her Clothes." *Pictures and Picturegoer* (March 4, 1933).

Naylor, Hazel Simpson. "Piloting a Dream Craft." *Motion Picture Magazine* (April 1921).

Nogueira, Roi. "I Am Not Going To Write My Memoirs." *Sight and Sound* (Spring 1969).

Nogueira, Roi, and Zalaffi, Nicoletta. "Entretien avec Gloria Swanson." *Cinema 71* (January 1971).

Parsons, Louella O. "The First True Life Story of Gloria Swanson." *Screenland* (January 1924).

———. "The Loves of Gloria Swanson." *Pictures and Picturegoer* (March 26–April 16, 1932.)

Peltret, Elizabeth. "Gloria Swanson Talks on Divorce." *Motion Picture Magazine* (December 1919).

Quirk, James R. "Everybody Calls Him 'Henry.' " *Photoplay* (June 1925).

Remont, Fritzi. "Diving into Drama." *Motion Picture Magazine* (December 1918).

———. "The Delightful Contradictions of Gloria." *Motion Picture Classic* (July 1919).

Rogers St. Johns, Adela. "The Confessions of a Modern Woman." *Photoplay* (February 1922).

———. "Gloria! An Impression." *Photoplay* (September 1923).

Smith, Frederick James. "The Silken Gloria." *Motion Picture Classic* (February 1920).

———. "Why I Am Going Back to the Screen." *Photoplay* (April 1937).

Smith, Helena Huntington. "Ugly Duckling." *New Yorker* (January 18, 1930).

Squier, Emma-Lindsay. "Milton plus Gloria and Eleanor." *Motion Picture Classic* (June 1921).

Swanson, Gloria. "A Week with the Stars: Wednesday." *Photoplay* (November 1921).

———. "What Is Love?" *Photoplay* (November 1924).

———. "There Is No Formula for Success." *Photoplay* (April 1926).

———. "My Most Wonderful Experience." *Photoplay* (February 1951).

Taylor, John Russell. "Swanson." *Sight and Sound* (Autumn 1968).

V. McC. "Gorgeous Gloria." *Pictures and Picturegoer* (May 1921).

Waterbury, Ruth. "Gloria, Connie and the Marquis." *Photoplay* (August 1930).

West, Myrtle. "The Price They Paid for Stardom." *Photoplay* (November 1926).

Wilde, Hagar. "Glamorous Gloria." *Talking Screen* (January 1930).

Anonymous. "Gloria Glorified." *Pictures and Picturegoer* (August 1918).

———. "A Photobiography of Gloria Swanson." *Photoplay* (June 1921).

———. "Gloria Speaks." *Pictures and Picturegoer* (October 1929).

Blanche Sweet

Ames, Courtney. "The Real Blanche Sweet." *Picture Play* (August 1916).

Bodeen, DeWitt. "Blanche Sweet." *Films In Review* (November 1965). *See also* issues of December 1965, February 1966, and June–July, October and November 1967.

Carr, Harry C. "Waiting for Tomorrow." *Photoplay* (May 1918).

———. "Three Little Girls Who Came Back." *Motion Picture Magazine* (August 1923).

———. "The Best-Known, Least-Known Girl." *Motion Picture Magazine* (January 1925).

Courtlandt, Roberta. "The Girl Who Reads Tennyson Between Scenes." *Motion Picture Magazine* (April 1916).

Ettinger, Margaret. "Impressions of Blanche and Micky." *Motion Picture Director* (February 1927).

Hall, Gladys. "Why Hollywood Marriages Fail." *Motion Picture Magazine* (February 1930).

Lederer, Josie, P. "Mr. and Mrs. Mickey." *Pictures and Picturegoer* (August 1924).

Owen, K. "The Girl on the Cover." *Photoplay* (April 1915).

Peltret, Elizabeth. "A Hilltop View." *Picture Play* (September 1918).

Rogers St. Johns, Adela. "An Impression of Blanche Sweet." *Photoplay* (September 1924).

Sherwood, C. Blythe. "Big Little Blanche." *Motion Picture Magazine* (December 1920).

Slide, Anthony. "Blanche Sweet and *Anna Christie*." *The Silent Picture* (Spring 1972).

Smith, Frederick James. "The New Blanche Sweet." *Motion Picture Classic* (November 1918).

Blanche Sweet and Marshall Neilan.

Blanche Sweet and Irene Rooke in Blanche's only British film, *The Woman in White* (1929).

Constance Talmadge.

Sweet, Blanche. "Conrad Nagel." *Photoplay* (June 1924).
———. "Keep Your Public Guessing." *Motion Picture Director* (August 1926).
———. "Judith of Bethulia." *The Silent Picture* (Winter 1969–1970).

Constance Talmadge

Bodeen, DeWitt. "Constance Talmadge." *Films In Review* (December, 1967). *See also* issues of January and December 1968.
Carr, Harry. "Connie Becomes a Chink." *Motion Picture Classic* (September 1922).
Courtlandt, Roberta. "Interviewing Constance." *Motion Picture Classic* (July 1918).
Goldbeck, Willis. "Tonsils and Terpsichore." *Motion Picture Magazine* (May 1922).
Hall, Gladys. "Name It!" *Motion Picture Magazine* (September 1920).
Kingsley, Grace. "The Wild Woman of Babylon." *Photoplay* (May 1917).
McGaffey, Kenneth. "Convalescing with Constance Talmadge." *Motion Picture Magazine* (April 1919).
Mackintosh, Capt. Alastair. *No Alibi*. London: Frederick Muller, 1961.
O'Reilly, Edward S. "A Date with Connie." *Photoplay* (September 1920).
Rogers St. Johns, Adela. "Matrimony and Meringues." *Photoplay* (July 1919).
Smith, Frederick James. "Tomboy Talmadge." *Motion Picture Magazine* (August 1919).
Talmadge, Constance. "What Am I?" *Motion Picture Magazine* (August 1918).
———"My Strangest Experience in the Movies." *Pantomime* (October 5, 1921).
———. "The Most Engaged Girl in the World." *Photoplay* (October 1923).
———. "What Is Love?" *Photoplay* (November 1924).
———"Why Men Fall in Love with Actresses." *Photoplay* (February 1925).
———. "Rire et Faire Rire." *Cinema Art* (November 1926).
Talmadge, Mrs. Margaret L. *The Talmadge Sisters*. Philadelphia: Lippincott, 1924.
Anonymous. "Constance Alice Talmadge." *Moving Picture World* (February 6, 1915).
———. "Constance Talmadge New Selznick Star." *Moving Picture World* (June 23, 1917).

Norma Talmadge

Carr, Harry. "Slumbering Fires." *Motion Picture Classic* (December 1922).
Carroll, Gardiner. "Why Norma Talmadge Avoids the Stage." *Photoplay* (July 1924).

Constance Talmadge as The Mountain Girl in *Intolerance* (1916).

Norma Talmadge.

Donnell, Dorothy. "She Loves and Lies." *Motion Picture Classic* (February 1920).

Fletcher, Adele Whitely. "Floating Island on Olympus." *Motion Picture Magazine* (March 1921).

Hall, Alice. "Talmadges Two." *Pictures and Picturegoer* (July 1921).

Hornblow, Arthur Jr. "Norma Talmadge." *Photoplay* (August 1915).

Lachmund, Marjorie Gleyre. "Our Norma." *Motion Picture Magazine* (January 1917).

Livingstone, Beulah. "Norma Talmadge—Queen of Versatility." *Photo-Play Journal* (March 1919).

MacDonald, Margaret I. "Norma Talmadge A Modern Female." *Moving Picture World* (July 21, 1917).

Naylor, Hazel Simpson. "That Tantalizing Talmadge." *Motion Picture Magazine* (October 1918).

O'Brien, Eugene. "Norma Talmadge." *Photoplay* (July 1924).

Old Timer, An. "Before They Were Stars: Norma Talmadge." *New York Dramatic Mirror* (April 17, 1920).

Rogers St. Johns, Adela. "The Lady of the Vase." *Photoplay* (September 1923).

———. "Our One and Only Great Actress." *Photoplay* (February 1926).

Service, Faith. "The Amazing Interview." *Motion Picture Classic* (January 1920).

Spears, Jack. "Norma Talmadge." *Films In Review* (January 1967). *See also* issues of February and March 1967 and February 1972.

Talmadge, Mrs. Margaret L. *The Talmadge Sisters.* Philadelphia: Lippincott, 1924.

Talmadge, Norma. "How Men Strike Me." *Photo-Play Journal* (March 1919).

———. "What 'Fashion' Really Means." *Photoplay* (June 1920).

———. "Eugene O'Brien." *Photoplay* (June 1924).

———. "Close-Ups." *Saturday Evening Post* (March 12, 1927).

———. "My Lucky Break." *Pictures and Picturegoer* (July 1928).

Vance, Elsie. "Norma Talmadge—the Adorable." *Photoplay* (February 1915).

Anonymous. "A Star in the Heaven of Celluloid." *Pictures and Picturegoer* (June 24, 1916).

———. "Compressed Careers No. 2: Norma Talmadge." *Pictures and Picturegoer* (February 1922).

Alice Terry

Barton, Ralph. "You Never Know Your Luck." *Photoplay* (October 1921).

Beach, Barbara. "Rex and His Queen." *Motion Picture Magazine* (January 1922).

Cheatham, Maude. "The Waking Beauty." *Motion Picture Classic* (July 1921).

Evans, Delight. "She Wants to Be Wicked." *Photoplay* (December 1922).

Howe, Herbert. "When Alice Played a German Soldier." *Photoplay* (February 1925).

Ingram, Mrs. Rex. "What Their Wives Say about Them." *Photoplay* (September 1923).

Johaneson, Bland. "Alice and Miss Terry." *Photoplay* (November 1924).

Novarro, Ramon. "Alice Terry." *Photoplay* (November 1924).

Terry, Alice. "Ramon Novarro." *Photoplay* (June 1924).

Anonymous. "About Alice." *Pictures and Picturegoer* (October 1928).

Florence Turner

Denig, Lynde. "Larry Trimble Brings Turner Films." *Moving Picture World* (August 12, 1916).

Hoffman, H. F. "Florence Turner Comes Back." *Moving Picture World* (May 18, 1912).

———. "Florence Turner Going to England." *Moving Picture World* (March 24, 1913).

Moen, L. C. "Florence Turner Returns to America." *Motion Picture News* (May 24, 1924).

Peltret, Elizabeth. "The Return of Florence Turner." *Motion Picture Classic* (February 1919).

Smith, Frederick James. "Unwept, Unhonored and Unfilmed." *Photoplay* (July 1924).

Trimble, Larry. "Concerning Florence Turner." *Moving Picture World* (December 6, 1913).

Turner, Florence. "Putting 'Move' into 'Movie.' " *Motion Picture Studio* (April 15, 1922).

Wilson, B. F. "Players of Yesteryear." *Motion Picture Classic* (July 1920).

Anonymous. "Miss Florence E. Turner: The Vitagraph Girl." *Moving Picture World* (July 23, 1910).

———. "Miss Florence Turner." *Pictures and Picturegoer* (June 6, 1914).

———. "American Players in England." *Moving Picture World* (July 18, 1914).

Rudolph Valentino

Arnold, Alan. *Valentino.* London: Hutchinson, 1952.

Bodeen, DeWitt. "Rudolph Valentino." *Screen Facts* (No. 17). *See also* issue No. 18.

Florence Turner.

Fulahn. "Was Valentino Poisoned?" *Pictures and Picturegoer* (January 1928).

F. W. F. "The Undying Valentino." *Motion Picture Director* (October 1926).

"George." "In Reply to Yours." *Pictures and Picturegoer* (May 1923).

Glyn, Elinor. "Rudolph Valentino as I Knew Him." *Modern Screen* (May 1931).

Goldbeck, Willis. "The Perfect Lover." *Motion Picture Magazine* (May 1922).

Hall, Alice. "Rudolph the Romantic." *Pictures and Picturegoer* (January 1922).

Holiday, Bertram. "Sheik and Son of Sheik." *Motion Picture Director* (July 1926).

Houston, Jane. "The Sheik Goes Hunting." *Cinema Art* (January 1926).

Huff, Theodore. "The Career of Rudolph Valentino." *Films In Review* (April 1952).

Lambert, Gavin. "Fairbanks and Valentino: The Last Heroes." *Sequence* (Summer 1949).

Lane, Wilton. "The Reason Why." *Pictures and Picturegoer* (September 1923).

Moderwell, Hiram Kelly. "When Rudy Was a Boy." *Photoplay* (January 1928).

Naldi, Nita. "Rudolph Valentino." *Photoplay* (June 1924).

Rudolph Valentino in *Monsieur Beaucaire* (1924).

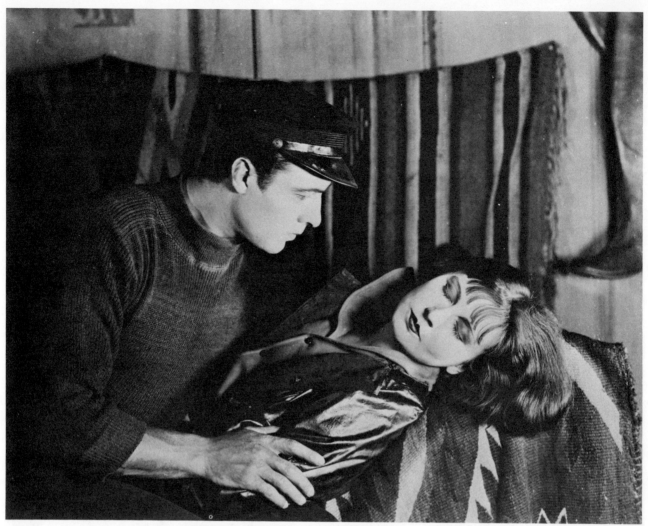

Rudolph Valentino and Dorothy Dalton in *Moran of the Lady Letty* (1922).

Newman, Ben-Allah. *Rudolph Valentino*. Hollywood: Ben-Allah Company, 1926.

Oberfirst, Robert. *Rudolph Valentino: The Man Behind the Myth*. New York: Citadel Press, 1962.

Peterson, Roger C. *Valentino, The Unforgiven*. Los Angeles: Wetzel, 1937.

Predal, René, and Florey, Robert. *Rudolph Valentino*. Paris: Anthologie de Cinéma, 1969.

Quirk, James R. "Presto Chango Valentino!" *Photoplay* (May 1925).

Rambova, Natacha. *Rudy*. London: Hutchinson, 1926.

Sherwood, C. Blythe. "Enter Julio." *Motion Picture Classic* (November 1920).

Shulman, Irving, *Valentino*. New York: Trident Press, 1967.

Smith, Frederick James. "Does Rudy Speak from the Beyond?" *Photoplay* (February 1927).

Steiger, Brad and Mank, Chaw. *Valentino*. NewYork: Macfadden-Bartell, 1966.

Tully, Jim. "Rudolph Valentino." *Vanity Fair* (October 1926).

Ullman, George S. *Valentino As I Knew Him*. New York: Macy-Masius, 1926.

Valentino, Rudolph. "Woman and Love." *Photoplay* (March 1922).

———. "An Open Letter from Valentino to the American Public." *Photoplay* (January 1923).

———. "My Life Story." *Photoplay* (February-April 1923).

———. *Daydreams*. New York: Macfadden Publications 1923.

———. *How You Can Keep Fit*. New York: Macfadden Publications, 1923.

———. "My Trip Abroad." *Pictures and Picturegoer* (July 1924–October 1925).

———. "What Is Love?" *Photoplay* (February 1925).

——. *My Private Diary*. Chicago: Occult Publishing Company, 1929.

——. *The Intimate Journal of Rudolph Valentino*. New York: William Faro, 1931.

Waterbury, Ruth. "Wedded and Parted." *Photoplay* (December 1922).

Winship, Mary. "When Valentino Taught Me to Dance." *Photoplay* (May 1922).

Lupe Velez

Albert, Katherine. "The Hot Baby of Hollywood, Otherwise Lupe Velez." *Photoplay* (February 1929).

Lupe Velez.

Busby, Marquis. "Lookee Lupe Whoopee!" *Photoplay* (March 1930).

Chute, Margaret. "Whoopee Lupe." *Pictures and Picturegoer* (September 5, 1931).

Dena, Walter, "What's Behind Lupe's Troubles." *Shadowplay* (October 1934).

Hamilton, Sara. "A Tornado? No, Lupe and Jimmy." *Photoplay* (December 1933).

Hampton, Jane. "Lupe and Johnny Were Lovers." *Photoplay* (June 1934).

Harrison, Helen. "You Can't Hold Your Man with Sex-Appeal." *Photoplay* (October 1934).

Lawton, Barbara. "Lupe—No Change!" *Photoplay* (December 1930).

L. C. "Lupe Velez." *Pictures and Picturegoer* (January 20, 1945).

Oettinger, Malcolm. "Just a Little Madcap." *Picture Play* (October 1929).

Anonymous. "Lupe Velez in an Ocean Adventure." *Pictures and Picturegoer* (April 23, 1932).

Florence Vidor

Carew, Olive. "Fame via Matrimony." *Motion Picture Classic* (February 1919).

Cheatham, Maude S. "The Wisdom of Contentment." *Motion Picture Classic* (February 1919).

Dunham, Harold. "Florence Vidor." *Films In Review* (January 1970). *See also* issue of October 1970.

Durling, E. V. "She Was the 'Girl Outside' Now She's 'Inside.' " *Photoplay* (August 1917).

Handy, Truman B. "Cobwebs of Convention." *Motion Picture Magazine* (March 1922).

Jordan, Joan. "Old Lives for News." *Photoplay* (April 1921).

Mistley, Media. "Florence Vidor Talks of Love and Other Things." *Motion Picture Magazine* (November 1918).

Oettinger, Malcolm H. "A Madonna among the Money-Changers." *Picture Play* (February 1925).

Rogers St. Johns, Adela. "Why Did the Vidors Separate?" *Photoplay* (August 1923).

——. "Why Has Florence Vidor Become the Toast of Hollywood?" *Photoplay* (August 1924).

——. "The Dissatisfied Beauty." *Photoplay* (April 1926).

Stacey, Maude. "Tea Time in the Garden." *Motion Picture Classic* (September 1921).

Vidor, Florence. "Marriage and a Screen Career Hazardous." *Theatre Magazine* (November 1927).

——. "How Marriage Helps a Movie Star." *Pictures and Picturegoer* (July 1921).

Vidor, King. "The Florence Vidor I Know." *Filmplay* (July 1922).

Florence Vidor and Ricardo Cortez in *The Eagle of the Sea* (1926).

George Walsh

Beach, Barbara. "The Gladiator of the Cinema." *Motion Picture Classic* (August 1919).

Blythe, Tony. "That Walsh Family." *Motion Picture Magazine* (November 1921).

Conley, Walter. "George Walsh." *The Silent Picture* (Summer–Autumn, 1971).

Naylor, Hazel Simpson. "Catching Up with George." *Motion Picture Magazine* (October 1918).

Slide, Anthony. "George Walsh Interview." *The Silent Picture* (Autumn 1972).

Henry B. Walthall

Cohn, Alfred A. "The Reformation of Wally." *Photoplay* (December 1917).

Gaddis, Pearl. "He Isn't the Little Colonel Any More." *Motion Picture Magazine* (September 1921).

George Walsh in *On the Jump* (1918).

Griggs, John. "Here Was an Actor!" *Films in Review* (March 1952).

Hall, Gladys. "The Little Colonel Carries On." *Motion Picture Magazine* (January 1929).

Jones, Gladys. "The Poe of the Screen." *Feature Movie Magazine* (January 1916).

Marple, Albert. "The Character Man of the Movies." *Motion Picture Classic* (February 1916).

McGaffey, Kenneth. "The New Walthall." *Motion Picture Magazine* (May 1919).

Owen, K. "The Little Colonel." *Photoplay* (August 1915).

Peltret, Elizabeth. "Walthall and the 'Little Colonel.'" *Motion Picture Classic* (November 1918).

Rankin, Ruth. "The Little Colonel Marches Back." *Photoplay* (June 1923).

Williamson, Edwin. "The Early Days of Henry B. Walthall." *Picture Play* (August 1916).

Wright, J. C. "Answering the Call." *Motion Picture Classic* (November 1922).

Anonymous. "Henry B. Walthall." *Moving Picture World* (January 10, 1914).

———. "Henry B. Walthall Joins Balboa." *Moving Picture World* (December 12, 1914).

Pearl White

Bacon, George Vaux. "The Girl on the Cover." *Photoplay* (January 1916).

Bruner, Frank V. "What Sort of a Fellow Is Pearl White?" *Photo-Play Journal* (February 1919).

———. "The Real Pearl White." *Motion Picture Magazine* (July 1919).

Condon, Mabel. "The Real Perils of Pauline." *Photoplay* (October 1914).

Davies, Wallace E. "Truth About Pearl White." *Films In Review* (November 1959).

Pearl White.

Eyck, John Ten. "Speaking of Pearls." *Photoplay* (September 1917).

Fletcher, Adele Whitely. "Reconsidering Pearl." *Motion Picture Magazine* (February 1921).

Hall, Alice. "The Ninety-Nine Lives of Pearl White." *Pictures and Picturegoer (February 1921).

Howe, Herbert. "A Star in Search of Her Soul." *Photoplay* (June 1923).

Johaneson, Bland. "Good-By Boys, I'm Through." *Photoplay* (April 1924).

Johnson, Julian. "The Girl on the Cover." *Photoplay* (April 1920).

Mitry, Jean. *Pearl White*. Paris: Anthologie du Cinema, 1969.

Mullett, Mary B. "The Heroine of a Thousand Dangerous Stunts." *American Magazine* (September 1921).

Naylor, Hazel Simpson. "All over the Plot at Pathe." *Motion Picture Magazine* (May 1918).

Sheridan, Oscar M. "Pearl in Paris." *Pictures and Picturegoer* (November 1923).

Smith, Frank Leon. "Pearl White and Ruth Roland." *Films In Review* (December 1960).

Smith, Frederick James. "A Pearl in the Rough." *Motion Picture Classic* (January 1919).

Stainton, Walter R. "Pearl White in Ithaca." *Films In Review* (May 1951).

Sterling, Ray. "Pearl White—Woman Wizard." *Photo-Play World* (May 1919).

Wade, Peter. "A Little of Everything—and Then Some More." *Motion Picture Classic* (January 1917).

Weltman, Manuel and Lee, Ray. *Pearl White: The Peerless, Fearless Girl.* South Brunswick and New York: A. S. Barnes and Company, 1969.

White, Pearl. "Putting It Over." *Motion Picture Magazine* (February 1917).

———. "Why I Like To Work for Uncle Sam." *Pictures and Picturegoer* (October 5, 1918).

———. *Just Me.* New York: George H. Doran, 1919.

Anonymous. "Pearl White." *Moving Picture World* (January 23, 1915).

———. "Always Just Escaping Death." *Pictures and Picturegoer* (July 27, 1918).

———. "Pearl White Number." *Pictures and Picturegoer* (June 28, 1919).

———. "Pearl White." *Pictures and Picturegoer* (October 9, 1920).

Thomas Meighan and Kathlyn Williams in *Conrad in Quest of His Youth* (1920).

Kathlyn Williams

Ames, Hector. "Kathlyn Williams Builder." *Motion Picture Magazine* (July 1916).

Burgess, Beth. "The Lady of the Lions Reconsiders." *Photoplay* (January 1917).

Carter, Aline. "Untouched by Ennui." *Motion Picture Magazine* (August 1921).

Denton, Frances. "Kathlyn's Memory Box." *Photoplay* (November 1917).

Howe, Herbert. "The Diplomat of Hollywood." *Photoplay* (September 1924).

Schmid, Peter Gridley. "An Animal Chat with Kathlyn Williams." *Motion Picture Classic* (January 1917).

Smith, Bertha H. "Nervy Movie Lady." *Sunset* (June 1914).

Lois Wilson

Cheatham, Maude. "Even as You and I." *Motion Picture Magazine* (December 1921).

Chic, Mlle. "What I Had To Learn in Pictures." *Moving Picture Weekly* (April 15, 1916).

Delvigne, Doris. "What's In a Name?" *Motion Picture Magazine* (August 1919).

Gassaway, Gordon. "Lois the Lovable." *Motion Picture Classic* (September 1922).

Lois Wilson still looked beautiful after her screen career was over.

Gladdis, Pearl. "The Girl Who Couldn't Be Discouraged." *Motion Picture Magazine* (May 1917).

Goldbeck, Willis. "A New Heroine for Barrie." *Motion Picture Magazine* (February 1921).

Johaneson, Bland. "Must She Commit Murder?" *Photoplay* (March 1924).

Rogers St. Johns, Adela. "Portrait of a Lady." *Photoplay* (April 1921).

Service, Faith. "You Can't Keep a Trouper Down." *Motion Picture Magazine* (September 1931).

Shelley, Hazel. "A Puritan in Pictures." *Motion Picture Classic* (September 1921).

Summers, Murray. "An Interview with Lois Wilson." *Filmograph* (Fall 1970).

Wilson, Lois. "What Is Love?" *Photoplay* (November 1924).

———. "A Letter from Location." *Picture Play* (February 1925).

———. "The Story of My Life." *Motion Picture Magazine* (April 1925).

———. "Bebe Daniels." *The Silent Picture* (Summer–Autumn 1971).

Anonymous. "Beauty Contestant Wins Her Wish." *Moving Picture World* (September 18, 1915).

———. "Lois Wilson." *Moving Picture World* (January 19, 1918).

Clara Kimball Young

Baker, Colgate. "The Girl on the Cover." *Photoplay* (May 1915).

Blaisdell, George F. "Clara Kimball Young, Artist." *Moving Picture World* (October 3, 1914).

Brewster, Eleanor. "The Age of Young." *Motion Picture Magazine* (March 1919).

Davis, Henry R. Jr. "Clara Kimball Young." *Films In Review* (August–September 1961). *See also* issue of October 1961.

MacDonald, Margaret I. "Clara Kimball Young Discusses Picture Art." *Moving Picture World* (July 21, 1917).

Peterson, Elizabeth. "The Divine Clara." *Motion Picture Classic* (June 1917).

Rudolph, W. H. "That Young Fondness for Animals." *Photo-Play Journal* (January 1919).

Squier, Emma-Lindsay. "The New Clara Kimball Young." *Motion Picture Classic* (December 1919).

Williamson, Agnes Bell. "A Screen Star's Hobby." *Filmplay Journal* (April 1922).

Young, Clara Kimball. "The Technique of Lovers." *Photoplay* (March 1920).

Anonymous. "Clara Kimball Young Discusses Reelism versus Realism." *Theatre* (February 1918).

———. "Making 'Savage Woman' Savage." *Pictures and Picturegoer* (August 2, 1919).

Clara Kimball Young.